First World War

and Army of Occupation

War Diary

France, Belgium and Germany

28 DIVISION
83 Infantry Brigade
Monmouthshire Regiment (Territorial Force)
3rd Battalion
4 August 1914 - 31 October 1915

WO95/2274/4

The Naval & Military Press Ltd
www.nmarchive.com
Published in association with The National Archives

Published by

The Naval & Military Press Ltd

Unit 10 Ridgewood Industrial Park,

Uckfield, East Sussex,

TN22 5QE England

Tel: +44 (0) 1825 749494

www.naval-military-press.com

www.nmarchive.com

This diary has been reprinted in facsimile from the original. Any imperfections are inevitably reproduced and the quality may fall short of modern type and cartographic standards.

Contents

Document type	Place/Title	Date From	Date To
Heading	WO95/2274/4		
Heading	28th Division 83rd Infy Bde 3rd Bn Monmouth Shire Regt Aug 1914-Sep 1915 To 49 Division (Pioneers)		
Heading	83rd Bde. War Diary Battalion Embarked For France 13.2.15. Joined 83rd Bde. Then In 5th Div 28.2.15. 3rd Monmouths August To December 1914 Sept 15		
War Diary	Abergavenny	04/08/1914	05/08/1914
War Diary	Pembroke Dock	06/08/1914	08/08/1914
War Diary	Pembroke Dock-Oswestry	09/08/1914	09/08/1914
War Diary	Oswestry	10/08/1914	29/08/1914
War Diary	Oswestry Northampton	30/08/1914	30/08/1914
War Diary	Northampton	31/08/1914	31/10/1914
War Diary	Grundisburgh	01/11/1914	13/11/1914
War Diary	Northampton	14/11/1914	30/11/1914
War Diary	Grundisburgh	01/12/1914	31/12/1914
Heading	83rd Bde. War Diary Disembarked Havre 15.2.15. Joined 83rd Bde. Then In 5th Div. 28.2.14. 3rd Monmouths January 1915		
War Diary		01/01/1915	31/01/1915
Heading	83rd Bde. War Diary Disembarked 15th February & Joined 83rd Bde. 5th Division 28.2.15. 3rd Monmouths February 1915		
War Diary		01/02/1915	28/02/1915
Heading	83rd Bde. 28th Div. War Diary Bde Temporarily Attached To 5th Division. 3rd Monmouths March 1915		
War Diary		01/03/1915	31/03/1915
Heading	Second Battle Of Ypres. April-May 1915. History Of The 3rd Monmouthshire Regiment		
Miscellaneous	3rd Monmouthshire Regiment.		
Heading	83rd Bde. 28th Div. Bde Left 5th Div & Rejoined 28th Div. 6.4.15. 3rd Monmouths April 1915		
War Diary		01/04/1915	29/04/1915
Miscellaneous	Chapter III. Second Battle Of Ypres-April-May 1915		
Heading	On His Majesty's Service.		
Diagram etc			
Miscellaneous			
Diagram etc			
Miscellaneous			
Diagram etc			
Miscellaneous			
Diagram etc			
Miscellaneous	Frezenberg Ridge Looking West		
Diagram etc			
Miscellaneous	3rd Monmouth Front Line		
Diagram etc			
Miscellaneous	3rd Monmouth Front Line		
Diagram etc			
Miscellaneous	Frezenberg Level Crossing Looking NNE		

Heading	83rd Bde. 28th Div. Amalgamated With 1st & 2nd Monmouths 27.5.15. & Became Part Of 84th Bde. 3rd Monmouths May 1915		
War Diary	Zonnegeeke	01/05/1915	08/05/1915
War Diary	Vlamertinghe	09/05/1915	09/05/1915
War Diary	Potijze	10/05/1915	10/05/1915
War Diary	Vlamertinghe	11/05/1915	11/05/1915
War Diary	Poperinghe	12/05/1915	13/05/1915
War Diary	Winnezeele	14/05/1915	22/05/1915
War Diary	Poperinghe	23/05/1915	23/05/1915
War Diary	Vlamertinghe	24/05/1915	27/05/1915
War Diary	Herseele	28/05/1915	28/05/1915
Heading	83rd Bde. 28th Div. War Diary Ceased To Be Amalgamated With 1st & 2nd Battalions After 11th August & Rejoined 83rd Bde As:- 3rd Monmouths August 1915		
Heading	On His Majesty's Service.		
War Diary	Lindenhoek	01/08/1915	02/08/1915
War Diary	Locre	03/08/1915	03/08/1915
War Diary	Kemmel	04/08/1915	06/08/1915
War Diary	Locre	07/08/1915	22/08/1915
War Diary	Kemmel	23/08/1915	28/08/1915
War Diary	Locre	29/08/1915	31/08/1915
Heading	83rd Bde. 28th Div. War Diary Became Pioneers To 49th Division 18.9.15. 3rd Monmouths September 1915		
War Diary	Locre	01/09/1915	04/09/1915
War Diary	Elverdinghe Chateau	05/09/1915	30/09/1915
Heading	Pioneers. 49th Division. Came From 83rd Bde. 28th Div. 18.9.15 3rd Monmouths October 1915		
Heading	On His Majesty's Service.		
War Diary	Elverdinghe Chateau	01/10/1915	31/10/1915

28TH DIVISION
83RD INFY BDE

3RD BN MONMOUTH SHIRE REGT

AUG ~~DEC~~ 1914-SEP 1915

To 49 DIVISION
(PIONEERS)

83rd Bde.

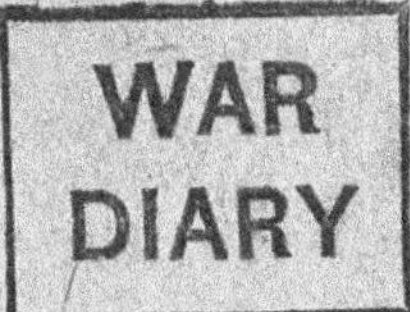

Battalion embarked for France 13.2.15.

Joined 83rd Bde. then in 5th Div 28.2.15.

3rd MONMOUTHS

AUGUST to DECEMBER

1 9 1 4

Sep '15

Instructions regarding War Diaries and Intelligence Summaries are contained in F. S. Regs., Part II. and the Staff Manual respectively. Title pages will be prepared in manuscript.

WAR DIARY
or
INTELLIGENCE SUMMARY.
(Erase heading not required.)

Army Form C. 2118.

Hour, Date, Place	Summary of Events and Information	Remarks and references to Appendices
4th Aug 1914. Abergavenny Tuesday	Order to mobilize at 5-10 p.m. Wires despatched to all Officers and Coys.	
5th Aug 1914 Abergavenny Wednesday	All Coys reported themselves at Headquarters Abergavenny during the course of the day. The total number being 2½% short of the strength of the Battalion. (The Battn (with two horses only) departed for Pembroke Dock 1st train 9.50 p.m 2nd train 10.50 p.m. Lieut [illegible] with advance party left for Pembroke Dock. Lieut Martin (horse purchaser) and Lieut Morton Jones transport Officer left for the horse purchasing area.	
6th Aug 1914 Pembroke Dock Thursday	(1) Arrived Pembroke Dock 1st train 1.20 a.m 2nd train 1.45 a.m.	
	(2) Major [illegible] left for Oswestry to take up duties R.T.O.	
	(3) Armed Guard furnished 1 Off. 68 men & 7 machine guns on H.M. Dockyard. 1 Off. & [illegible] men Wireless Station	
	(4) Battn. – Part – routine & training. Remainder – clearing round, digging [illegible] Pembroke	
7th Aug 1914 Pembroke Dock Friday	(1). Lieut R. A. [illegible] and advance party left for Oswestry at 7.30 a.m.	
	(2) Battn: Part – Routine and training. Remdr – clearing round, digging trenches near Pembroke	

(73989) W4141—463. 400,000. 9/14. H.&J.Ltd. Forms/C. 2118/10.

2

Instructions regarding War Diaries and Intelligence Summaries are contained in F. S. Regs., Part II. and the Staff Manual respectively. Title pages will be prepared in manuscript.

WAR DIARY
or
INTELLIGENCE SUMMARY.
(*Erase heading not required.*)

Army Form C. 2118.

Hour, Date, Place	Summary of Events and Information	Remarks and references to Appendices
8th Aug 1914 Saturday	1 Battn - Routine and training.	
9th Aug 1914 Sunday Pembroke Dock - Oswestry	(1) Batt left Pembroke Dock (via Neyland) for Oswestry and were relieved by the 3rd S W B (SR). 1st train (½ Battn + 2 horses). 7.30 a m 2nd train ([illegible]) 8.30 a m and arrived at Oswestry 1st train 2.15 p m 2nd train 3.25 p m (2) Batt. billeted as follows (a) 5 Coys the Cross Market (b) 3 Coys the National School Headquarters: Queen Hotel.	
10th Aug 1914 Oswestry	(1) Battn Routine + training (2) Capt Evans + Baker + Lieut Brown with 84 men joined from the Depot.	
11th Aug 1914 Oswestry	(1) Battn Routine + training (2) The 6 Coys billeted at the Cross Market changed billets as follows (a) 5½ Coys to The Boys Secondary School (b) ½ Coy to The Roman Catholic School (3) Bounties paid	

(73989) W4141—463. 400,000. 9/14. H.&J.Ltd. Forms/C. 2118/10.

3

Instructions regarding War Diaries and Intelligence Summaries are contained in F. S. Regs., Part II. and the Staff Manual respectively. Title pages will be prepared in manuscript.

WAR DIARY
or
INTELLIGENCE SUMMARY.
(Erase heading not required.)

Army Form C. 2118.

Hour, Date, Place	Summary of Events and Information	Remarks and references to Appendices
12th Aug 1914 Oswestry	(1) Battln Routine & training. Brigade Duty (2) The Brigade was paraded and addressed by the Brigadier who made a stirring appeal to the Brigade to Volunteer for service abroad, a full report of this appeal appeared in the local papers (3) Lieut Martin & Merion Jones with the transport [illegible] one water cart and 35 men arrived	
13th Aug 1914 Oswestry	(1) Battln - Routine and training (2) The Brigadier visited billetts (3) Lieut Brown sent home sick (4) Batt Headquarters moved from Queens Hotel to the Boys Secondary Schools	
14 Aug 1914 Oswestry	(1) Inspected by Major-Gen Lindley G O C Welsh Div Exercise - the attack of position, 2 Coys in firing line 2 Coys one on each flank 4 Coys in Reserve. Commended (2) Capt Evans proceeded to the Depot to relieve W A Lewis	

(73989) W4141—463. 400,000. 9/14. H.&J.Ltd. Forms/C. 2118/10.

Instructions regarding War Diaries and Intelligence Summaries are contained in F. S. Regs., Part II. and the Staff Manual respectively. Title pages will be prepared in manuscript.

WAR DIARY
or
INTELLIGENCE SUMMARY.
(*Erase heading not required.*)

Army Form C. 2118.

Hour, Date, Place	Summary of Events and Information	Remarks and references to Appendices
15 Aug 1914 Oswestry	(1) Battn. 1st line transport practised entraining & detraining by day and night. By day:- Entraining 35 minutes. Detraining 10 minutes. By night, Entraining 11 minutes Detraining 8 minutes (2) Routine & training (3). Battn inspected by M.O. (4) The Rev J R Phillips ([illegible] 6th W Glams Chaplain) Capt Evans & 2 English Natl Reserve and 6 men arrived from Depot	
16 Aug. 1914 Oswestry.	(1) The Battn attended the Brigade Church Parade at Cae Glas Park (2) Battn on Brigade duty	
17 Aug 1914 Oswestry	(1) Routine & Training (2) In consequence of a message received from the caretaker at the Oswestry Local Water Supply & no officer at the time being found at the Brigade office, a guard consisting of 1 N.C.O & 3 men was found for the water supply	

(73989) W4141—463. 400,000. 9/14. H.&J.Ltd. Forms/C. 2118/10.

Instructions regarding War Diaries and Intelligence Summaries are contained in F. S. Regs., Part II. and the Staff Manual respectively. Title pages will be prepared in manuscript.

WAR DIARY
or
INTELLIGENCE SUMMARY.
(*Erase heading not required.*)

Army Form C. 2118.

Hour, Date, Place	Summary of Events and Information	Remarks and references to Appendices
18th Aug 1914 Oswestry	(1) Routine and Training (2) Brigade informed that a total of 817 has volunteered for service abroad	
19th Aug 1914 Oswestry	(1) Routine and training	
20th Aug 1914 "	(1) Routine and training. (2) The Battn practised entraining and detraining and day and night	
21 Aug 1914 "	(1) Routine & training (2) Lieuts Gathe & Gorman promoted to Captains	
22 Aug 1914 "	(1) Routine and training (2) moved from billets to Camp at The old Show Grounds Oswestry. (3). Coys equalized	
23 Aug 1914 "	(1). The Battn attended Brigade Church Parade at Cae Glas Park	
24 Aug 1914	(1). Routine and training	

(73989) W4141—463. 400,000. 9/14. H.&J.Ltd. Forms/C. 2118/10.

Army Form C. 2118.

Instructions regarding War Diaries and Intelligence Summaries are contained in F. S. Regs., Part II. and the Staff Manual respectively. Title pages will be prepared in manuscript.

WAR DIARY
or
INTELLIGENCE SUMMARY.
(Erase heading not required.)

Hour, Date, Place	Summary of Events and Information	Remarks and references to Appendices
25 Aug 1914 Oswestry	1. Routine and training 2. Brigade Order that the transport wagons of the Battn carry Green and White flags 3. Lieut Reed appointed acting Signalling Officer " Wilson " Scout	
26 Aug 1914 "	1 Routine and training	
27 Aug 1914 "	1 Routine and training	
28 Aug 1914 "	1 Routine and training 2 The Brigade Comr published a valedictory order in relation to the numbers in the Brig who had volunteered for service abroad and a telegram was also received from Major Gen The Hon J Lindley on the same subject (Garrison Order No 8) (3). Lieut R A Lewis with an advance party left for Northampton.	
29 Aug 1914 "	(1) Routine and training	

(73989) W4141—463. 400,000. 9/14. H.&J.Ltd. Forms/C. 2118/10.

7

Instructions regarding War Diaries and Intelligence Summaries are contained in F. S. Regs., Part II. and the Staff Manual respectively. Title pages will be prepared in manuscript.

WAR DIARY
or
INTELLIGENCE SUMMARY.
(Erase heading not required.)

Army Form C. 2118.

Hour, Date, Place	Summary of Events and Information	Remarks and references to Appendices
30 Aug 1914 Oswestry Northampton	1. Struck camp and returned camp equipment to Ordnance 2. The Battn moved from camp at ~~[illegible]~~ Oswestry to billets at Northampton 1st train left 2.50 p m arrived at 7.50 p m 2nd " " 4.50 p m 9.50 p m	
31 Aug 1914 Northampton	1. Routine and training 2. Army Order – All leave stopped & troops now being on active service powers of C.O. in dealing with offences as laid down by the Army Act can be legally enforced	

(73989) W4141—463. 400,000. 9/14. H.&J.Ltd. Forms/C. 2118/10.

8

Instructions regarding War Diaries and Intelligence Summaries are contained in F. S. Regs., Part II. and the Staff Manual respectively. Title pages will be prepared in manuscript.

WAR DIARY
or
INTELLIGENCE SUMMARY.
(*Erase heading not required.*)

Army Form C. 2118.

Hour, Date, Place	Summary of Events and Information	Remarks and references to Appendices
1st Sept 1914. Northampton	1. Routine & training 2. Court of Enquiry (Capt Williams [illegible] Routledge & [illegible]) held on 18 absentees who were struck off the strength. 3. [illegible] Whitehead and 84 men joined from the Depot. 4. Battn on Brigade Duty.	
2. Sept 1914. Northampton	1. Routine and training	
3 Sept 1914 "	1. Routine and training 2 Inspection by the Gen Off Comd 1st Army Central Force Gen Sir Bruce Hamilton 3. Major Fawkes appointed member of Board on Rifle Range	
4. Sept 1914 "	1 Routine and training	
5. Sept 1914 "	1. Bde Route march via Duston [illegible] [illegible] & Upton leaving starting point (Cop. Tramway Terminus Kingsley Rd) at 9. a.m. and returned at 2. p.m. 2 Battn on Brigade Duty. The following officers having reported themselves were posted as follows [illegible] [illegible] C Co [illegible] [illegible] B Co	

9

Instructions regarding War Diaries and Intelligence Summaries are contained in F. S. Regs., Part II. and the Staff Manual respectively. Title pages will be prepared in manuscript.

WAR DIARY
or
INTELLIGENCE SUMMARY.
(*Erase heading not required.*)

Army Form C. 2118.

Hour, Date, Place	Summary of Events and Information	Remarks and references to Appendices
6. Sept 1914 Northampton	1 Brigade Church Parade at Victoria Park 2 Col Ford interviewed by the Brigadier and informed that he would shortly be called upon to take over command of the Reserve Battn and Officer of the Regular Army to be appointed to command this Battn.	
7 Sept 1914 Northampton	1. Routine and training 2 Medical Inspection of men who have vol^d for Foreign Service 3 1/2 half Battn Bathing 4. Capt Cookson Lieut Wilson Lieut O'Connor, Sergt Brig Powell & Sergt Restall returned to Depot	
8 Sept 1914 "	1 Routine and training. 2 Medical Inspection of men who have vol^d for service abroad continued 3 Col Ford received orders to take command of the Reserve Battn 4 2/Lts Newman & Whitehead & Groves in this days London Gazette	

Army Form C. 2118.

WAR DIARY
or
INTELLIGENCE SUMMARY.
(Erase heading not required.)

Instructions regarding War Diaries and Intelligence Summaries are contained in F. S. Regs., Part II. and the Staff Manual respectively. Title pages will be prepared in manuscript.

Hour, Date, Place	Summary of Events and Information	Remarks and references to Appendices
9 Sept 1914 Northampton	1 Routine and training 2 Medical Inspection of men who have vol^d for service abroad continued 3. Col [illegible] left to take command of Reserve Batt Major [illegible] being placed in temporary command of this Batt^n 4 Batt^n on Brigade Duty	
10 Sept 1914	1. Routine and training 2. The M.O lectured the Batt^n on the advisability of innoculation against typhoid and strongly urged every man to be innoculated 3 Published in this days orders that as from the 1st Sept 1914 a kit allowance of 2^d per day would be credited to the account of all N.C.Os & men	
11 Sept 1914	1 Routine and training. The Battalion marched to its area for inspection by Genl Sir Bruce Hamilton but the Genl only saw Batt^n on its way back to billets	

(73989) W4141—463. 400,000. 9/14. H.&J.Ltd. Forms/C. 2118/10.

10.

Instructions regarding War Diaries and Intelligence Summaries are contained in F. S. Regs., Part II. and the Staff Manual respectively. Title pages will be prepared in manuscript.

WAR DIARY
or
INTELLIGENCE SUMMARY.

(*Erase heading not required.*)

Army Form C. 2118.

Hour, Date, Place	Summary of Events and Information	Remarks and references to Appendices
12 Sept 1914. Northampton	1. Brigade Route march via Duston thence via cross roads to the Towcester Road and back 2. Published in Orders that as from the 14th the Marching Order is to [illegible] all parades except those for Physical Exercise 3. Brig Genl Heme met with a regrettable accident just prior to the start of the Brigade Route march	
13 Sept 1914. "	1. Brigade Church Parade at Victoria Park 2. Memo. received at 1 pm that Capt Worsley Gough (late Connaught Rangers) had been appointed (subject to sanction) to command the Battn 3. Volunteers from the right ½ Battn innoculated against typhoid	
14 Sept 1914 "	1. Battn on Brigade Duty 1. Routine and training	
15 Sept 1914	1. Routine and training 2. Pte J Ellis 1504 died at the Civil Hospital Northampton	

(73989) W4141—463. 400,000. 9/14. H.&J.Ltd. Forms/C. 2118/10.

Instructions regarding War Diaries and Intelligence Summaries are contained in F. S. Regs., Part II. and the Staff Manual respectively. Title pages will be prepared in manuscript.

WAR DIARY
or
INTELLIGENCE SUMMARY.
(Erase heading not required.)

Army Form C. 2118.

Hour, Date, Place	Summary of Events and Information	Remarks and references to Appendices
16 Sept 1914. Northampton	1 Routine and training 2 Volunteers from left half Battn inoculated against typhoid 3. Lt Col Wooley Gough arrived at 5 pm and had a conference with Officers 4 Pte J Ellis A Coy (see entry the 15th) is struck off the strength	
17 Sept 1914 "	1 Routine and training	
18 Sept 1914 "	1 Routine and training	
19 Sept 1914 "	1 Battn Route march without arms or ammunition 2. Lieut R A Lewis detailed as Battn Billeting Officer	
20 Sept 1914 "	1 Brigade Church Parade at Victoria Park	

(73989) W4141—463. 400,000. 9/14. H.&J.Ltd. Forms/C. 2118/10.

12

Instructions regarding War Diaries and Intelligence Summaries are contained in F. S. Regs., Part II. and the Staff Manual respectively. Title pages will be prepared in manuscript.

WAR DIARY
or
INTELLIGENCE SUMMARY.
(*Erase heading not required.*)

Army Form C. 2118.

Hour, Date, Place	Summary of Events and Information	Remarks and references to Appendices
21 Sept 1914 Northampton	1 Routine and training 2 Major Fawkes proceeded to Depot to take over Stores and Books for the Battn 3 Lieut & QM Martin appointed Asst Adjutant 5/8/14 4 The following being unfit are struck off the strength No 987 L/Cpl W Bevan C Coy 1820 Pte A Sweet A Coy 5 Innoculation for further detachment including stewards, grooms, clerks orderlies, cooks etc	
22 Sept 1914 "	1 Routine & Training	
23 Sept 1914 "	1 Routine & Training 2 The Officers and men innoculated on 13th inst innoculated for the 2nd time 3 Capt Baker is attached from duty with Reserve Battn from this date 4 Sergt Instr J Hatton appointed acting Sergt Major from this date 5 The following being unfit struck off strength No 1631 Pte Owen C Coy	

(73989) W4141—463. 400,000. 9/14. H.&J.Ltd. Forms/C. 2118/10.

13

Instructions regarding War Diaries and Intelligence Summaries are contained in F. S. Regs., Part II. and the Staff Manual respectively. Title pages will be prepared in manuscript.

WAR DIARY
or
INTELLIGENCE SUMMARY.
(Erase heading not required.)

Army Form C. 2118.

Hour, Date, Place	Summary of Events and Information	Remarks and references to Appendices
21 Sept 1918 Northampton	1 Routine and training 2 The following being medically unfit struck off strength: 1895 Pte W J Boulton B Coy	
25 Sept 1918	1 Routine & training	
26 Sept 1918	1 Route march (less those Officers & men to be innoculated) 2 The Officers & men inoculated of the 16th were inoculated for the 2nd time	
27 Sept 1918	1 Brigade Church Parade at Victoria Park	
28 Sept 1918	1 Routine & Training. Company training commencing on this date	
29 Sept 1918	1 Routine & Co training 2 2nd Lieut [illegible] joined the Battn and posted to F Coy	

(73989) W4141—463. 400,000. 9/14. H.&J.Ltd. Forms/C. 2118/10.

1/1

WAR DIARY
or
INTELLIGENCE SUMMARY.
(Erase heading not required.)

Army Form C. 2118.

Instructions regarding War Diaries and Intelligence Summaries are contained in F. S. Regs., Part II. and the Staff Manual respectively. Title pages will be prepared in manuscript.

Hour, Date, Place	Summary of Events and Information	Remarks and references to Appendices
30 Sept 1914 Wednesday Northampton	1. Routine & Coy training	
	2. Major C. Bishop detailed to report at No. [illegible] Army (Central Force) at Bedford [illegible] for temporary duty with the General Staff	
	3. Extract from London Gazette [illegible]/9/14 to be 2/Lieuts:	
	Gerald W. Lawrence	
	John Porter Worton	
	Maurice Headland Sifton	
	Reginald Morris Sifton	
	4. The following being medically unfit for further service proceed to Depot on 30/9/14	
	A Coy Pte Gough 1346 Murphy 1535 Reid 1785	
	B Coy Pte Davies 1870 Morgan 1428	
	D Coy Pte Morgan 1720 Thompson 1453	
	E Coy Pte Rackley 1586	
	G Coy Sergt Pickering 136 Pte Davies 1488	

Instructions regarding War Diaries and Intelligence Summaries are contained in F. S. Regs., Part II. and the Staff Manual respectively. Title pages will be prepared in manuscript.

WAR DIARY
or
INTELLIGENCE SUMMARY.
(*Erase heading not required.*)

Army Form C. 2118.

Hour, Date, Place	Summary of Events and Information	Remarks and references to Appendices
1 Oct 1914	Omission Sep 23rd Major W. S. Bridge late (D.L.I.) joined the Battalion as 2nd in Command. Company Training	
2 Oct 1914	Retreat - Advanced 1-5.30 p.m. 2/Lt R. M. Derry reported for duty and was taken on the strength of the Battalion. Lecture to Officers of Batt by Capt Leardy 9th Gurkhas Gen Staff on "The conduct of the attack"	
3 Oct 1914	Brigade Tactical Exercise. Advance Guard, A Coy 3 Batt Mon Regt under Major W. S. Bridge	
5 Oct 1914	Company training	
6 Oct 1914	Company training. 8 Rec. Officers 95 recruits proceeded to Tamworth for a Recruits course of musketry	
7 Oct 1914	Divisional Route march via Kettering Rd Overstone Pk returning to Northampton	

(73989) W4141—463. 400,000. 9/14. H.&J.Ltd. Forms/C. 2118/10.

16

Instructions regarding War Diaries and Intelligence Summaries are contained in F. S. Regs., Part II. and the Staff Manual respectively. Title pages will be prepared in manuscript.

WAR DIARY
or
INTELLIGENCE SUMMARY.
(Erase heading not required.)

Army Form C. 2118.

Hour, Date, Place	Summary of Events and Information	Remarks and references to Appendices
8 Oct 1914	Battalion found working Party - 1 Officer 2 N.C.Os & 6 men for Dallington range. No 2352 Pte M. A. Sifton having been gazetted as 2Lt is struck off strength of Battalion	
9 Oct 1914	Company training	
10 Oct 1914	Boots inspected by 2nd in Command. Battalion Route march	
12 Oct 1914	Company training. 2 Coys Miniature Range Practise	
13 Oct 1914	Company training. 2 Coys. Miniature Range Practise. Capt & Adj Smithers was granted Sick Leave. Capt [illegible] appointed A/Adj in his place	
14 Oct 1914	Company training. 2 Coys Miniature Range Practise. Order (Brigade) issued relative to the use of only Official Books & publications for training	

Army Form C. 2118.

Instructions regarding War Diaries and Intelligence Summaries are contained in F. S. Regs., Part II. and the Staff Manual respectively. Title pages will be prepared in manuscript.

WAR DIARY
or
INTELLIGENCE SUMMARY.

(*Erase heading not required.*)

Hour, Date, Place	Summary of Events and Information	Remarks and references to Appendices
15 Oct 1914	Exercise of Battalion in digging trenches upon a selected position (Glass Thorpe Hill) Hours of work 9 a m to 4 p m. Lecture to all Officers on Entrenching by C R E.	
16 Oct 1914	Exercise of Battalion in conjunction with 1st and 2nd Batt Mon Regt in attack of Entrenched position (Glass thorpe Hill)	
17 Oct 1914	93 recruits proceeded to Tamworth for a Recruits course of musketry	
18 Oct 1914	Times of Reveille & Retreat altered to 6 a m and 5 p m respectively	
19 Oct 1914	Company training 2 Coys miniature Range Practise Extract from London Gazette 20 Oct 1914 "Captain Worsley [illegible] Reserve of Officers to be Lt. Col. (Temporary) dtd 10 Sept 1914	
20 Oct 1914	Company training, Scouts & Cyclists Sections at miniature Range practise	

Instructions regarding War Diaries and Intelligence Summaries are contained in F. S. Regs., Part II. and the Staff Manual respectively. Title pages will be prepared in manuscript.

Army Form C. 2118.

WAR DIARY
or
INTELLIGENCE SUMMARY.
(Erase heading not required.)

Hour, Date, Place	Summary of Events and Information	Remarks and references to Appendices
21 Oct 1914	Tactical Exercise by Battalion - Attack from position on Road Pitsford - Brampton Street - Market Harboro Road on Spratton Orders relative the training of "Observers"	
22 Oct 1914	Company training - & Coys miniature Range Prac.	
23 Oct 1914	Tactical Exercise by the Brigade - Attack by Brigade from Duston to a point in Althorpe Park.	
24 Oct 1914	Company training & Coys miniature Range Practise Officers (Brigade) Conference under the B. G. C. on tactical Exercise of previous day	
25 Oct 1914	Lecture by a/Adjutant on Conduct of Range practises to all Officers and N. C. Os	
26 Oct 1914	Musketry Practise on Billington Range by ½ Battalion - Batt duty & Companies & musketry training & Companies	
27 Oct 1914	musketry training.	

(13989) W4141—463. 400,000. 9/14. H.&J.Ltd. Forms/C. 2118/10.

Army Form C. 2118.

Instructions regarding War Diaries and Intelligence Summaries are contained in F. S. Regs., Part II. and the Staff Manual respectively. Title pages will be prepared in manuscript.

WAR DIARY
or
INTELLIGENCE SUMMARY.
(*Erase heading not required.*)

Hour, Date, Place	Summary of Events and Information	Remarks and references to Appendices
28 Oct 1918.	Musketry Practise at Dallington Range by ½ the Battalion	
29 Oct 1918	Musketry training. Capt. J. T. C. Williams proceeded to Abergavenny to take over duty as Depot Officer there.	
30 Oct 1918	Musketry Practise on Dallington Range by Casuals of Battalion. Medical Inspection of 2nd/4 Battalion by R. M. Officer.	
31 Oct 1918	The Battalion proceeded to Ipswich by Rail and to* Tuddenham by march route where it was billeted for the night. A party of 2 N. C. O.s 20 men and 78 recruits left at Northampton as Details – Lt Routledge & 2/Lt Bennett being left as in Commands of details & billeting Officers respectively. *(and surrounding Villages)	

Army Form C. 2118.

Instructions regarding War Diaries and Intelligence Summaries are contained in F. S. Regs., Part II. and the Staff Manual respectively. Title pages will be prepared in manuscript.

WAR DIARY
or
INTELLIGENCE SUMMARY.
(*Erase heading not required.*)

Hour, Date, Place	Summary of Events and Information	Remarks and references to Appendices
1st Nov 1914 Sunday Grundisburgh.	The Battalion proceeded by march route to Grundisburgh where it was billetted	
2nd Nov 1914.	The Battalion was employed in the digging of defensive Trenches. The right of section allotted the Battalion resting on Squitch Wood and facing NE extending to Grundisburgh. Mens dinners cooked in the field	
3 Nov 1914	Digging of Defensive trenches continued - 8.30am to 4pm Haversack Rations - Dinners on return to billetts Lecture to N.C.Os by Coy Comdrs in Evening	
4 Nov 1914	Digging of Defensive Trenches continued 8.30 am to 4 pm	
5 Nov 1914	Digging of Def. trenches continued 8.30am to 4 pm	
6 Nov 1914	Digging of Def Trenches contd 2 Coys employed same ground 2 Coys " Carr Farm. 8.30 am to 4 pm	

(73989) W4141—463. 400,000. 9/14. H.&J.Ltd. Forms/C. 2118/10.

Instructions regarding War Diaries and Intelligence Summaries are contained in F. S. Regs., Part II. and the Staff Manual respectively. Title pages will be prepared in manuscript.

WAR DIARY
or
INTELLIGENCE SUMMARY.
(Erase heading not required.)

Army Form C. 2118.

Hour, Date, Place	Summary of Events and Information	Remarks and references to Appendices
7 Nov 1914 Grundisburgh	Digging of Def: Trenches Contd Companies employed on former ground as finished moving on to Park Farm 8-30 a.m to 4 p.m	
8 Nov 1914 "	Digging of Def: trenches contd 8-30 a.m to 4 p.m	
9 Nov 1914 "	Digging of Def: trenches continued. 8-30 a.m to 4 p.m Arrangements were made for an Orderly to be always at Grundisburgh to receive and at once communicate to Hd Qrs of the Battalion any telephone messages. Capt L T C Williams was transferred to Reserve Battn and Lt [illegible] to the Depot at Abergavenny to relieve him as Depot Officer. All Bayonets of the Battalion were sharpened locally by smiths in the village of Grundisburgh	
10 Nov 1914	Digging of Def: trenches round Green Hill Farm 8 a.m to 4 p.m. A Free issue of one pair of woollen pants to all N.C.O. and men was made	

(73989) W4141—463. 400,000. 9/14. H.&J.Ltd. Forms/C. 2118/10.

Instructions regarding War Diaries and Intelligence Summaries are contained in F. S. Regs., Part II. and the Staff Manual respectively. Title pages will be prepared in manuscript.

WAR DIARY
or
INTELLIGENCE SUMMARY.
(Erase heading not required.)

Army Form C. 2118.

Hour, Date, Place	Summary of Events and Information	Remarks and references to Appendices
11 Nov 1914 Grundisburgh	Digging of Def Trenches contd 9 a.m. to 4 p.m. Breakfast before leaving billetts - dinners and teas on return to billetts - Orders received to hold in readiness to proceed to India. Embarking on 23 Nov 1914	
12 Nov 1914	Digging of Def. Trenches contd meals as on 11th inst 9 a.m. - 4 p.m.	
13 Nov 1914	Battalion proceeded by rail to Northampton - by ½ Batt at the time.	
14 Nov 1914 Northampton	A Roll call of Batt. was made 9 a.m. at Northampton. Special instructions were issued to all Officers as to kit etc to be obtained for India. Leave (48 hrs) granted to 6 Coys of the Batt. to proceed home. Retreat altered to 4.30 p.m. Reveille " " 6.30 a.m.	
15 Nov 1914	Parades for Divine Service for various denominations. All leave stopped and all on leave recalled	
16 Nov 1914	Special Instructions issued to Officers for an emergency move of Batt. in Field Drill	

(73989) W4141—463. 400,000. 9/14. H.&J.Ltd. Forms/C. 2118/10.

Instructions regarding War Diaries and Intelligence Summaries are contained in F. S. Regs., Part II. and the Staff Manual respectively. Title pages will be prepared in manuscript.

WAR DIARY
or
INTELLIGENCE SUMMARY.
(*Erase heading not required.*)

Army Form C. 2118.

Hour, Date, Place	Summary of Events and Information	Remarks and references to Appendices
17 Nov 1914 Northampton	Divisional precautionary instructions received for march by road to Cambridge. Physical Training for Battalion in Drill Field Inspection of all Rifles by tomorrow. Nominal Rolls of men to proceed to India called for and received into Hd Qrs of the Batt Major W J Bridge proceeded to Tuddenham to take over command of the Brigade Details which left behind at Grundisburgh and Witnesham vice Major Williams 3rd Batt. R Welsh Fusiliers. Capt W A Lewis also proceeded to Grundisburgh to take charge of the details of the 3rd Batt. Northants Reg.	
18 Nov 1914	B. C. E & H. Companies Field table C. part 3 appendix 1. M. Dallington Range. A. Coy. Butt duty D F & G Coys – Company training. Helmets were procured on Indent for all N.C.Os and men who are under orders to proceed to India	
19 Nov 1914	Physical Exercise for all Units of the Batt. The musketry training for all Units of Batt. under their own Comdrs. Recruits and Recruits Officers performed Recruits course of musketry on Dallington Range 9.30. am – 1 p m 6 Officers & 55 N.C.Os & men attended the memorial Service of F M Earl Roberts held at Northampton to represent the Battalion.	

Instructions regarding War Diaries and Intelligence Summaries are contained in F. S. Regs., Part II. and the Staff Manual respectively. Title pages will be prepared in manuscript.

WAR DIARY
or
INTELLIGENCE SUMMARY.
(Erase heading not required.)

Army Form C. 2118.

Hour, Date, Place	Summary of Events and Information	Remarks and references to Appendices
20 Nov 1914 Northampton	Physical Exercise of all Units of Batt. Recruits performed Recruits musketry course on Dallington Range. Lectures were given in the Evening as follows:- All Sergeants under Sergt-major. Coy Scouts under Coy Officer. Coy training under O.C. Companies.	
21 Nov 1914	6 boys performed the trained mens course musketry on Dallington Range. One boy on Butt Duty Certificates were obtained from O.C. Companies that all men under their command to proceed to India were fully clothed and equipped. The whole of the Recruits of the Battn were inspected by the Brig. Genl. Commdg. 2/Lt Somerset was detailed as a member of D.C. martial held at Northampton 22 Nov 1914	
22 Nov 1914	Divine Service, Medical Inspection of the Batt.	
23 Nov 1914	Physical Exercise, Coy Drill and musketry training for trained men under Coy Comdrs. Recruits, Junior Officers & selected N.C.O.s under the Sergt major for [illegible] Batt Drill Field Specialists under their own Officers for instruction Instructions in duties of Patrol Leaders for all Sec Comdrs under Co. Comdrs and for Corporals under the Sergt major.	

(3989) W4141—463. 400,000. 9/14. H.&J.Ltd. Forms/C. 2118/10.

Instructions regarding War Diaries and Intelligence Summaries are contained in F. S. Regs., Part II. and the Staff Manual respectively. Title pages will be prepared in manuscript.

WAR DIARY
or
INTELLIGENCE SUMMARY.
(Erase heading not required.)

Army Form C. 2118.

Hour, Date, Place	Summary of Events and Information	Remarks and references to Appendices
24 Nov 1914. Northampton	Parades same as 23rd. Special Batt. order, as to the non wearing of flags & unauthorized Badges - & Caps being worn on the head - also as to various existing faults in Saluting, Sentries Etc. All Rifles that had been noted as miss firing on range, were taken to the Armourers Shop - Instructor of Musketry also attended for report	
25 Nov 1914	6 Companies performed part of trained mens Course of musketry on Dallington Range. One Coy acting on Butt duty. Recruits were drilled by Sergt-Major on Drill Field - Junior Officers also attended this parade. Special orders issued in Batt. Orders as to the orders regarding moves destinations being *confidential*. Revised Rolls of N.C.O's & men who are to proceed to India were issued and ordered to be read out on 3 consecutive parades. Major W. Jones R.A.M.C. was relieved by Lt Col. McKean R.A.M.C. and was struck off the strength of the Batt.	

(73989) W4141—463. 400,000. 9/14. H.&J.Ltd. Forms/C. 2118/10.

Instructions regarding War Diaries and Intelligence Summaries are contained in F. S. Regs., Part II. and the Staff Manual respectively. Title pages will be prepared in manuscript.

WAR DIARY
or
INTELLIGENCE SUMMARY.
(*Erase heading not required.*)

Army Form C. 2118.

Hour, Date, Place	Summary of Events and Information	Remarks and references to Appendices
26 Nov Northampton	Physical Exercise & Coy training - musketry & Visual training under Coy Officers - Recruits & Junior Officers under Sergt Major. Lectures were given as under To Coy Scouts by O.C. Companies & C/Sergts by Sergt Major To specialists under their own Officers	
27 Nov 1914 "	Physical training - musketry training for Recruits under Sergt Major. married men were left at the disposal of O.C. Companies for the purpose of checking and inspecting kits Equipment & Rifles - Lectures in the Evening as follows - to corporals by Sergt Major to selected N.C.Os by O.C. Companies To specialists by their own officers	
28 Nov 1914	Physical training Coy Drill under O.C. Coys. Recruits & selected N.C.Os under Sergt Major 2.30 p.m. Coys were left at the disposal of O.C. Coys for Inspection of Equipment etc Extract from London Gazette appeared in Western Com^d Orders 23.11.14 3rd Batt Monmouthshire Regt W.S. Bridge (late Capt DL1) to be Major dated 23 Sept 1914	

Instructions regarding War Diaries and Intelligence Summaries are contained in F. S. Regs., Part II. and the Staff Manual respectively. Title pages will be prepared in manuscript.

WAR DIARY
or
INTELLIGENCE SUMMARY.
(*Erase heading not required.*)

Army Form C. 2118.

Hour, Date, Place	Summary of Events and Information	Remarks and references to Appendices
29. Nov 1914. Northampton	1. Divine Services	
	Extract from London Gazette d/d 25 Nov 1914.	
	3rd Batt Northns Regt Lieuts to be Captains - W Pawledge J Lancaster to date from 1 Nov 1914.	
	Western Comd Orders (Extract from)	
	The following Extract from London Gazette d/26.11.14 is published for information	
	Major J. Bishop 4th Northns Regt T.F in succession to Capt Co Place D.S.O R.E of 6 Oct 1914	
	To be General Staff Officers 3rd Grade.	
30. Nov 1914	Battalion proceeded by rail (½ Batt at a time) to Woodbridge Suffolk and thence by march route to Grundisburgh. Each man fully equipped carrying his kit bag with 2nd suit Service Dress - Spare shirts, socks & Boots & necessary small kit - Waterproof Sheet in coat carriers.	
	Haversack rations carried. Officers baggage limited to 35 lbs. Surplus Officers Kits - Barrack Equipment - Practice Ammunition - Surplus stores etc stored at St James Institute Northampton	
	Capt O W G Steel was left in charge of Batt Details* together with Lieut W McGregor, G Bennett & 2/Lt Sorby	
	* Details consisted of 190 Recruits	

Army Form C. 2118.

Instructions regarding War Diaries and Intelligence Summaries are contained in F. S. Regs., Part II. and the Staff Manual respectively. Title pages will be prepared in manuscript.

WAR DIARY
or
INTELLIGENCE SUMMARY.
(*Erase heading not required.*)

Hour, Date, Place	Summary of Events and Information	Remarks and references to Appendices
1st Dec 1914. Grundisburgh	Work resumed on defence works.	
2nd Dec 1914	Work on the entrenchments continued	
3rd " 1914	Work on the entrenchments continued	
4th " 1914	Work on the entrenchments continued Central Force Orders received inviting applications from Junior Officers for transfer to R.F.C. names of following sent in Lt Bennett Lt Grooves 2/Lt Onions 2/Lt Sorby	
5 Dec 1914	Work on Entrenchments continued. Following Extract from Central Force Orders dated 2.12.14 was published in Battn Orders "The G.O.C. in Chief has much pleasure in publishing the following extract from a report by the Deputy Director of Railway transport of the Central Force An Entrainment at Northampton (18 trains) conveying two Brigades of the Welsh Divisn took place on the 30th November between 12.30 am and 9 a.m. The Troops concerned were the Welsh Border & N. Wales Brigade. The movement was most satisfactorily carried out, all troops arrived the entraining station punctually, despite the Dreary rain and the inclemency of the weather. The loading was carried out Expeditiously and, in every case but one, the train started before time in spite of difficulties owing	

(73989) W4141—463. 400,000. 9/14. H.&J.Ltd. Forms/C. 2118/10.

Instructions regarding War Diaries and Intelligence Summaries are contained in F. S. Regs., Part II. and the Staff Manual respectively. Title pages will be prepared in manuscript.

WAR DIARY
or
INTELLIGENCE SUMMARY.
(Erase heading not required.)

Army Form C. 2118.

Hour, Date, Place	Summary of Events and Information	Remarks and references to Appendices
5th Dec 1914 (Cont)	to the short type of carriage truck provided. The detrainment at Ipswich, Newmarket, Needham, and Woodbridge was also carried out in a soldierly and workman like manner and all the circumstances strengthen the opinion that an emergency move on a larger scale may be carried out successfully.	
6 Dec 1914	Work on the Entrenchments continued	
7 Dec 1914	Work on the Entrenchments continued. The following extract from the London Gazette was published for information. Lieuts to be Captains:- R. A. Lewis R. O. Gardner. 2nd Lts to be Lieuts. G. E. Tyler L. E. Whitehead F. A. Groves. to date from 23-11-14	
8 Dec 1914	Work on the Entrenchments continued.	
9 Dec 1914	Work on the Entrenchments continued. Colour Sergt W. M. Porter is appointed Quarter Master Sergt as from 28-11-14	
10 Dec 1914	Work on the Entrenchments continued.	

(73989) W4141—463. 400,000. 9/14. H.&J.Ltd. Forms/C. 2118/10.

WAR DIARY
or
INTELLIGENCE SUMMARY.
(Erase heading not required.)

Army Form C. 2118.

Instructions regarding War Diaries and Intelligence Summaries are contained in F. S. Regs., Part II. and the Staff Manual respectively. Title pages will be prepared in manuscript.

Hour, Date, Place	Summary of Events and Information	Remarks and references to Appendices
11 Dec 1914	Work in the Entrenchments cont^d	
12 Dec 1914	Work in the Entrenchments cont^d. Sergt Major Hatton detailed to superintend a course of instruction of N.C.O.s at Northampton. Col. Sergt Lippiatt took on duties of A/Sr Maj	
13 Dec 1914	The H^d Qrs & remainder of Welsh Border Bde having proceeded to Bury St Edmunds on 11th inst the battalion took over the whole section of defences from Woodbridge to [illegible] and the Coy billets were changed and distributed along the line. H^d Qrs remaining at [illegible]	
14 Dec 1914	Work on Entrenchments cont^d	
15 Dec 1914	Work on Entrenchments cont^d	
16 Dec 1914	Work in Entrenchments cont^d	
17 Dec 1914	Work in Entrenchments cont^d	
18 Dec 1914	Work in Entrenchments cont^d	
19 Dec 1914	Work in Entrenchments cont^d	

(73989) W4141—463. 400,000. 9/14. H.&J.Ltd. Forms/C. 2118/10.

Instructions regarding War Diaries and Intelligence Summaries are contained in F. S. Regs., Part II. and the Staff Manual respectively. Title pages will be prepared in manuscript.

WAR DIARY
or
INTELLIGENCE SUMMARY.
(Erase heading not required.)

Army Form C. 2118.

Hour, Date, Place	Summary of Events and Information	Remarks and references to Appendices
20 Dec 1914	Church Parade under Coy arrangements. Major W. S. Bridge proceeded to Northampton to take charge of Bde Details on Musketry	
21 Dec 1914	Work in Entrenchments contd	
22 Dec 1914	Work in Entrenchments contd	
23 Dec 1914	Work in Entrenchments contd	
24 Dec 1914	Work in Entrenchments contd	
25 Dec 1914	Christmas Day	
26 Dec 1914	Work in Entrenchments contd	
27 Dec 1914	Church Parade under Coy arrangements	
28 Dec 1914	Work in the Entrenchments Contd	
29 Dec 1914	Work in the Entrenchments Contd	
30 Dec 1914	Work in the Entrenchments Contd	
31 Dec 1914	Work in the Entrenchments Contd	

83rd Bde.

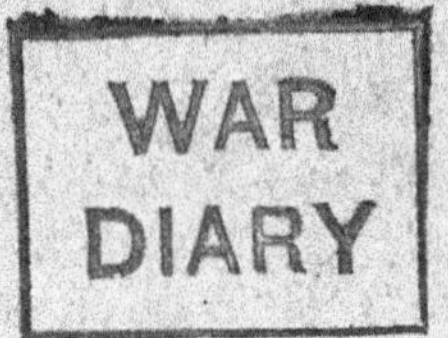

Disembarked Havre 15.2.15.

Joined 83rd Bde. then in 5th Div. 28.2.15.

3rd MONMOUTHS

JANUARY

1915

Instructions regarding War Diaries and Intelligence Summaries are contained in F. S. Regs., Part II. and the Staff Manual respectively. Title pages will be prepared in manuscript.

WAR DIARY
or
INTELLIGENCE SUMMARY.
(Erase heading not required.)

Army Form C. 2118.

Hour, Date, Place	Summary of Events and Information	Remarks and references to Appendices
1 Jan 1915	Work in Entrenchments continued.	
2 Jan 1915.	Work Contd. The following Extract from Bde Orders was published in Battn. Orders "The Brig. General Comdg in wishing all ranks the best of Good luck health and happiness in the New Year now seizes the opportunity to express his warm appreciation of the Good Work done in the trenches and the General Good Conduct of the Brig during the past two months. He has been deeply impressed by the heartiness and willingness with which the work had been carried out under the very depressing weather that have prevailed during the [illegible] of this period. The discomfort experienced by [illegible] in the extreme the cold and wet and in trenches sometimes full of water, and on the water logged ground, being billeted in open barns at this season of the year have all been borne with the cheerfulness, good humour and adaptability to circumstances so characteristic of the British soldier. All this augurs well for the future and inspires a confidence that the Battalions of this Brigade will give a good account of themselves whenever they are	

(73989) W4141—463. 400,000. 9/14. H.&J.Ltd. Forms/C. 2118/10.

Instructions regarding War Diaries and Intelligence Summaries are contained in F. S. Regs., Part II. and the Staff Manual respectively. Title pages will be prepared in manuscript.

WAR DIARY
or
INTELLIGENCE SUMMARY.
(*Erase heading not required.*)

Army Form C. 2118.

Hour, Date, Place	Summary of Events and Information	Remarks and references to Appendices
2 Jan 1916	called upon to do sterner work, and endure great hardships and privations in the presence of the enemy. He feels sure that all will continue to work hard and seize every opportunity to improve in every way so as to make themselves thoroughly efficient and fit to take the field when called upon to do so with credit to themselves their Battalions & honour to their King & Country	
3 Jan 1915	Sunday	
4 Jan 1915	Entrenchment work continued. Extracts from a report from General H^d Qrs Exped. Force on certain points noticed on the arrival of Territorial Units at the front were published in Batt Orders	
5 Jan 1915	Entrenchments cont^d	
6 Jan 1915	Entrenchment work cont^d	
7 Jan 1915	General tidying up of the lines of Entrenchments and collection of tools & technical stores	
8 Jan 1915	Collection of tools continued.	

(73989) W4141—463. 400,000. 9/14. H.&J.Ltd. Forms/C. 2118/10.

Instructions regarding War Diaries and Intelligence Summaries are contained in F. S. Regs., Part II. and the Staff Manual respectively. Title pages will be prepared in manuscript.

WAR DIARY
or
INTELLIGENCE SUMMARY.
(Erase heading not required.)

Army Form C. 2118.

Hour, Date, Place	Summary of Events and Information	Remarks and references to Appendices
9 Jan 1916	General cleaning up of billets, further collection of tools, storing of tools, technical stores etc. Route Orders issued for Cambridge	
10 Jan 1916	Batt proceeded by Rail to Cambridge. Major Bridge and musketry details of the battalion rejoined from Northampton	
11 Jan 1916	Coys under Coy Commanders carried out Physical Exercise, Saluting drill.	
12 Jan 1916	"The Four Coy Organisation" was adopted for tactical and drill purposes. Steady Drill Platoons Coy. Special Orders were issued in Batt orders as to walking out dress, the proper way of wearing Great Coats when in the streets & prohibiting the wearing of handkerchiefs and sweaters in a way to show above the uniform. Miniature Range Practice was carried out by 1 Company per day - 1 Platoon at a time	
13 Jan 1916	Steady Drill - Platoon & Coy.	
14 Jan 1916	Steady Drill - Platoon & Coy	

(73989) W4141—463. 400,000. 9/14. H.&J.Ltd. Forms/C. 2118/10.

Instructions regarding War Diaries and Intelligence Summaries are contained in F. S. Regs., Part II. and the Staff Manual respectively. Title pages will be prepared in manuscript.

WAR DIARY
or
INTELLIGENCE SUMMARY.
(*Erase heading not required.*)

Army Form C. 2118.

Hour, Date, Place	Summary of Events and Information	Remarks and references to Appendices
15 Jan 1915	Steady drill, Platoon & Coy. Lecture to all Coys by the Sergt Major in the training. Retreat was altered to 5.30 p.m. Re-sighted Rifles (to Mark VII am) issued and the old rifles returned to Ordnance.	
16 Jan 1915	Brigade Route March about 11 Miles	
17 Jan 1915	Selection of this Battalion with others for Overseas	
18 Jan 1915	Steady Drill - also walking out & saluting also Guard duties. Lecture in musketry to all Sergts by Lt Abbots on his return from Musketry School at Bisley	
19 Jan 1915	Steady Drill, Batt, Coy & Platoon. The desirability of inoculation before proceeding abroad explained to all those men who have as yet not been so treated. Lectures to 10 selected men per double Coy on Elementary Musketry each afternoon by Lt Abbots. New clothing issued to double Coy at a time. Extension of hours up to which soldiers of the Welsh Divn may be on licensed Premises - to 9 p.m.	

(73989) W4141—463. 400,000. 9/14. H.&J.Ltd. Forms/C. 2118/10.

Instructions regarding War Diaries and Intelligence Summaries are contained in F. S. Regs., Part II. and the Staff Manual respectively. Title pages will be prepared in manuscript.

WAR DIARY
or
INTELLIGENCE SUMMARY.
(*Erase heading not required.*)

Army Form C. 2118.

Hour, Date, Place	Summary of Events and Information	Remarks and references to Appendices
20 Jan 1915	Divisional Route march and inspection by C. in Chief Central Force. Full marching order 50 rds SAA on each man. Transport packed and loaded. About 9 miles march & march past in Fours – Column of Route	
21 Jan 1915	Steady Drill, Batt Coy Platoon. Saluting, Setting up & General Smartness in walking out dress	
22 Jan 1915	Steady Drill Batt Coy Platoon. Further inoculation of men who have as yet not been treated	
23 Jan 1915	Steady Drill – Saluting & General Smartness in walking out	
24 Jan 1915	5 Officers & 250 men Rank & File proceeded on Special Leave — 4 days —	
25 Jan 1915	Steady Drill Musketry Instruction to selected Officers & N C Os. Lecture to all Corporals on Musketry by last returned Officer from Bisley School of M.	
26 Jan 1915	Steady Drill Lecture for all Sergts on Transport duties by Transport Officer	

Instructions regarding War Diaries and Intelligence Summaries are contained in F. S. Regs., Part II. and the Staff Manual respectively. Title pages will be prepared in manuscript.

WAR DIARY
or
INTELLIGENCE SUMMARY.
(Erase heading not required.)

Army Form C. 2118.

Hour, Date, Place	Summary of Events and Information	Remarks and references to Appendices
27 Jan 1915	Steady Drill setting up & general smartness in walking out drill. About 350 officers Rank & File proceeded on Special Leave 3 days. A [illegible] Coy was exercised in Falling in in the Dark and taking off & putting on Equipment. The following C.O. in Chief's remarks were published in Central Force Orders of 23 Jan 15. "The C. O. in Chief wishes to express his keen appreciation of the soldierly spirit which has animated all Ranks of the Central Force during the preparation by them of defensive positions. The weather has been atrocious, the billets, barns & out houses in which the troops have been perforce located & are often inconveniently situated. The clay in which they delved was the Genuine English Clay. During these adverse conditions some 200 miles of trenches have been dug, the Equivalent of a continuous line stretching from London to Liverpool. Many miles of barbed wire Entanglements have been erected as well as a great number of gun emplacements communication trenches and redoubts. The enthusiasm of the Central Force made light work of it as well as the discomforts. Neither flood nor mud has been able to damp their ardour [illegible] though it has [illegible] Foe	

(73989) W4141—463. 400,000. 9/14. H.&J.Ltd. Forms/C. 2118/10.

Instructions regarding War Diaries and Intelligence Summaries are contained in F. S. Regs., Part II. and the Staff Manual respectively. Title pages will be prepared in manuscript.

WAR DIARY
or
INTELLIGENCE SUMMARY.
(*Erase heading not required.*)

Army Form C. 2118.

Hour, Date, Place	Summary of Events and Information	Remarks and references to Appendices
27 Jan 1915 (Continued)	as a test nothing could be of better augury for the future, and once more the General officer Comdg. in chief [illegible] those serving under him of his recognition of their energy and conduct	
28 Jan 1915	Musketry – on University Range by recruits and trained men of C Coys Specialists and employed also firing M. G. Practice was carried out on Coldham Range. An Instructional course of Lectures to selected Officers on Transport Duties was given by Transp. Officer.	
29 Jan 1915	Musketry on University Range was continued. The remainder of the Batt not on leave performed Steady Drill. A Class of Instruction was held for N.C.Os by S. Major Howard O.T.C. at which selected N.C.Os of the Batt attended.	
30 Jan 1915	Musketry on University Range contd [illegible] "C" Coys and recruits fired. Route March by Coys. 4 Coys Organization came into effect for all purposes from this date:– A.F. = A Coy Comdr Capt [illegible] B.C. = B Coy Comdr Capt W Rutledge E.G. = C Coy Commdr Capt O. W. D. Steel D.H. = D Coy Comdr Capt W [illegible] A Draft of 120 men arrived from Reserve Batt.	

Instructions regarding War Diaries and Intelligence Summaries are contained in F. S. Regs., Part II. and the Staff Manual respectively. Title pages will be prepared in manuscript.

WAR DIARY
or
INTELLIGENCE SUMMARY.
(Erase heading not required.)

Army Form C. 2118.

Hour, Date, Place	Summary of Events and Information	Remarks and references to Appendices
31 Jan 1915.	Musketry on University Range contd by recruits. The draft of 120 men was placed temporary under the command of Capt Tyler, Lt Abbott and selected N.C.Os. Extract from London Gazette 26/1/15 Lieut A. Tyler to be Captain (Temporary). dated Oct 2 - 2/Lt Derry to be Lieut (Temporary) dated 2 Oct/1914.	

(73989) W4141—463. 400,000. 9/14. H.&J.Ltd. Forms/C. 2118/10.

83rd Bde.

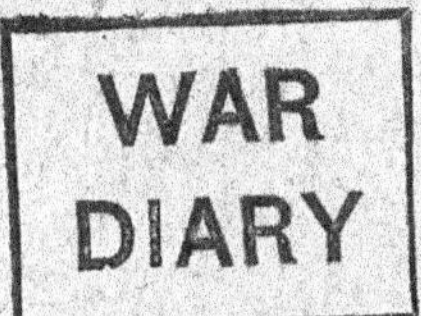

Disembarked 15th February & joined 83rd Bde.
5th Division 28.2.15.

3rd M O N M O U T H S

F E B R U A R Y

1 9 1 5

Instructions regarding War Diaries and Intelligence Summaries are contained in F. S. Regs., Part II. and the Staff Manual respectively. Title pages will be prepared in manuscript.

WAR DIARY
or
INTELLIGENCE SUMMARY.
(*Erase heading not required.*)

Army Form C. 2118.

Hour, Date, Place	Summary of Events and Information	Remarks and references to Appendices
1st Feb 1915	Musketry on University Range continued. Recruits fired	
2nd Feb 1915	Route marching by Coys under their own Commanders	
3. Feb 1915	Musketry on University Range. Route marching of Battn by Coys	
4 Feb 1915	Steady Drill by Coys. Receipt of Equipment and Ammunition. Commencement of issue by Coys. Arrival of Armourer Sergt and overhaul of Rifles by Coys commenced	
5 Feb 1915	Steady Drill, musketry for recruits on Range. Issue of Equipment Contd	
6 Feb 1915	Battn placed at Disposal of Coy Commdrs for fitting and adjustment of Equipment. Inspection of Transport and fitting of Saddlery by O.C. A.S. Corps.	
7 Feb 1915	Sunday	

Instructions regarding War Diaries and Intelligence Summaries are contained in F. S. Regs., Part II. and the Staff Manual respectively. Title pages will be prepared in manuscript.

WAR DIARY
or
INTELLIGENCE SUMMARY.
(Erase heading not required.)

Army Form C. 2118.

Hour, Date, Place	Summary of Events and Information	Remarks and references to Appendices
8 Feb 1915	Fitting and Adjustment of Equipment continued Kit Inspection by Coy Commdrs.	
9 Feb 1915.	Fitting & Adjustment of Equipment Continued.	
10 Feb 1915.	Fitting & Adjustment of Equipment Continued. Definite orders as to Departure of Batt for Overseas received Divisional parade – for rehearsal of His Majesty's inspection.	
11 Feb 1915.	His majesty the King visited and inspected the Division The Division was formed up on Parker's Piece under Maj Genl The Rght Hon. J E Lindley who received his majesty – Royal Salute. His majesty inspected the troops and the troops then marched past in double fours. His majesty spoke to each of the Comdg officers who were proceeding abroad.	
12 Feb 1915	The Batt paraded with 1st Mon Regt in Kings College Lawn and received a farewell speech from the Officer Comdg the Welsh Divn Major Gen the Rgt J E Lindley the Welsh Border Inf Brig. Brigadier Genl J Hume	

(73989) W4141—463. 400,000. 9/14. H.&J.Ltd. Forms/C. 2118/10.

Instructions regarding War Diaries and Intelligence Summaries are contained in F. S. Regs., Part II. and the Staff Manual respectively. Title pages will be prepared in manuscript.

WAR DIARY
or
INTELLIGENCE SUMMARY.
(Erase heading not required.)

Army Form C. 2118.

Hour, Date, Place	Summary of Events and Information	Remarks and references to Appendices
13 Feb 1915	The Batt proceeded by rail to Southampton and embarked on S.S. Chyebassa [illegible] 500 men & remainder of Batt on other Transports.	
14 Feb 1915.	The above transports sailed for France at 8.15 p.m.	
15 Feb 1915.	Arrived at Havre 9 a.m. The Batt marched up to Rest Camp at St Addresse - and was encamped there in tents for the night.	
16 Feb 1915.	The Batt proceeded by rail from there at 8 p.m.	
17 Feb 1915	Arrived at Cassell about 5 p.m. and marched from Station to town under heavy rain and was billetted for the night. The Transport remaining at Station	
18 Feb 1915	The Batt proceeded by march Route to Steenvoorde the transport proceeding by lower route around hill - and was billetted in that Village	
19 Feb 1915.	Trench Digging & Route march by Coys. 2/Lt [illegible] and 1 O.R. 600 men proceeded for trench work around Ypres	

(73989) W4141—463. 400,000. 9/14. H.&J.Ltd. Forms/C. 2118/10.

Instructions regarding War Diaries and Intelligence Summaries are contained in F. S. Regs., Part II. and the Staff Manual respectively. Title pages will be prepared in manuscript.

WAR DIARY
or
INTELLIGENCE SUMMARY.
(*Erase heading not required.*)

Army Form C. 2118.

Hour, Date, Place	Summary of Events and Information	Remarks and references to Appendices
20. Feb 1915.	Trench Digging by Battalion	
21 Feb 1915	Long Route march by Batt and carried out Advance under Artillery Fire and attack practice.	
22 Feb 1915	Trench Digging by Battalion	
23 Feb 1915	Repetition of the 21st inst The Battalion was visited by Major Gen Sir A. Hunter	
24 Feb 1915	Route march by Battalion. Inspection of Batt and Address to Officers by General Sir H. Smith Dorrien The Battalion performed night trench digging from 7.30 to 9.30 p.m. digging themselves in, with also Communication trenches to shelter Trenches in the time.	
25 Feb 1915	Battalion Route march finished by improving & draining trenches made on previous night	
26 Feb 1915	Battalion Route march, advance & Rear Guards In the Evening the Battalion was practised in manning & relieving of Trenches in the Dark,	

Instructions regarding War Diaries and Intelligence Summaries are contained in F. S. Regs., Part II. and the Staff Manual respectively. Title pages will be prepared in manuscript.

WAR DIARY
or
INTELLIGENCE SUMMARY.
(*Erase heading not required.*)

Army Form C. 2118.

Hour, Date, Place	Summary of Events and Information	Remarks and references to Appendices
27 Feb 1915	Battalion Route March. Officers & N.C.O. instructions by R.E. in detonators & the throwing of bombs and hand grenades.	
28 Feb 1915	Batt proceeded by march route to Caestre from whence it embussed (motor) to Bailleul where it was billeted at St Jans Capell.	

(73989) W4141—463. 400,000. 9/14. H.&J.Ltd. Forms/C. 2118/10.

83rd Bde.
28th Div.

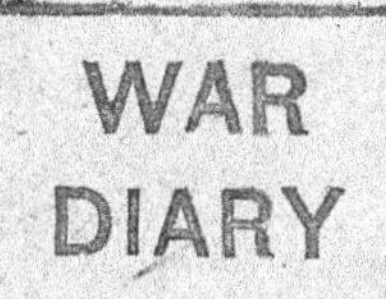

Bde temporarily attached to 5th Division.

3rd M O N M O U T H S

M A R C H

1 9 1 5

Instructions regarding War Diaries and Intelligence Summaries are contained in F. S. Regs., Part II. and the Staff Manual respectively. Title pages will be prepared in manuscript.

WAR DIARY
or
INTELLIGENCE SUMMARY.
(Erase heading not required.)

Army Form C. 2118.

Hour, Date, Place	Summary of Events and Information	Remarks and references to Appendices
1 March 1915	Batt proceeded by Rout March to Ravelsberghe and was there billeted. The C.O. 6 Officers + 16 N.C.O.s proceeded for 24 hours daily instruction in the trenches. Coys were placed at disposal of Commdrs for Inspection + General clearing up. Lts Whitehead + Hodges underwent instruction in Bomb throwing & Grenades	
2 March 1915.	Coys at disposal of Commdrs for Inspec. + General clearing up. Selected Bomb Throwers instructed by Lts Hodges & Whitehead	
3 March 1915.	Coys at disposal of Commdrs. Major Bridges + 7 other officers proceeded for 24 hours duty (instructional) in the trenches.	
4 March. 1915	A + B Coys proceeded for 24 hrs duty (instructional) in the trenches.	
5 March 1915	C Coy proceeded for 24 hrs duty instructional in the trenches	

Instructions regarding War Diaries and Intelligence Summaries are contained in F. S. Regs., Part II. and the Staff Manual respectively. Title pages will be prepared in manuscript.

WAR DIARY
or
INTELLIGENCE SUMMARY.
(*Erase heading not required.*)

Army Form C. 2118.

Hour, Date, Place	Summary of Events and Information	Remarks and references to Appendices
6 March 1915	All Officers attended a lecture on "Observation of Artillery" in Bailleul conference of C Comdrs with Major Genl R Boyle Comdg 83rd Brigade to which Brigade the Batt has now been posted. D Coy proceeded for 24 hrs duty (instrumental) in the trenches	
8 March 1915.	D Coy to trenches for Fatigue work carriage of R.E. stores. Report received that 2/Lt Lancaster had been promoted whilst on Trench Work near Ypres.	
9 March 1915	2 Platoons of A Co in trenches attached to Y&L Regt Visited by Major Genl Boyle and congratulated on their work	
11 March 1915	Conference with all Officers of the Batt with Major Genl Boyle. 2 Platoon A Coy attached Y&L Regt	
12 March 1915	Battalion proceeded to the trenches (10A & 10B) for duty 500 yds frontage. Battalion Base shifted to Dranoutre & 10A & 10B supports.	

(73989) W4141—463. 400,000. 9/14. H.&J.Ltd. Forms/C. 2118/10.

Army Form C. 2118.

Instructions regarding War Diaries and Intelligence Summaries are contained in F. S. Regs., Part II. and the Staff Manual respectively. Title pages will be prepared in manuscript.

WAR DIARY
or
INTELLIGENCE SUMMARY.
(*Erase heading not required*.)

Hour, Date, Place	Summary of Events and Information	Remarks and references to Appendices
13 March 1915	No 1 Supporting Points and [illegible] [illegible] garrisons were [illegible] posted at [illegible] [illegible] Bde Hd Qrs at St Quentin [illegible] B & C Coys occupied fire trenches [illegible] March to night of 5th March D Coy relieved C Coy [illegible]	3 [illegible]
15 March 1915	2 Platoons of A Coy under Capt R. A. [illegible] Cont the Batt 4th [illegible] Dug-Outs near St Quentin No 391 Dr Mandell was wounded in the Finger by Gun Shot whilst in the left end of A's trench No 1390. Pte A. Pocock received G. S. W through right in same trench and end - A's No 935 Pte A J Parsons received G. S. W in ankle 1471 Sgt Deacon recd G. S. W. in left leg	
16 March 1915	Battalion was under orders to be relieved by the 7th Brigade on this night but was cancelled and remained for the night on duty 1593 Pte Ranscombe recd G. S. W back of head 1/6 [illegible] recd G. S. W in left temple, brought to Dressing station same night - serious case 2196 Pte G Williams recd fatal G. S. W in neck, brought down that night and was buried at St Quentin next morning Lt Mallen R A M C reading the Burial Service over the Grave	

(73989) W4141—463. 400,000. 9/14. H.&J.Ltd. Forms/C. 2118/10.

WAR DIARY
or
INTELLIGENCE SUMMARY.
(*Erase heading not required.*)

Army Form C. 2118.

Instructions regarding War Diaries and Intelligence Summaries are contained in F. S. Regs., Part II. and the Staff Manual respectively. Title pages will be prepared in manuscript.

Hour, Date, Place	Summary of Events and Information	Remarks and references to Appendices
17 march 1915	Batt was relieved by 5th K.O. R.L. Regt in the evening – proceeded by march route to Dranoutre [illegible] it was billetted in Huts. 2/Lt Whitehead whilst putting up a false parapet in B10 trench recd a S.W. through the thigh – was brought down to Dressing Station & Left in Ambulance.	3 [illegible]
18 march 1915	The Battalions was exercised in Physical Drill and Steady Coy Drill.	
19 & 20 march 1915	Same as above	
21 march 1915	Sunday – The Battalion attended Divine Service in Field opposite Batt Orderly Room. Later 1.30 Batt proceeded by march route to Ravelsburgh and was then billetted in its old Billets of March 1–12	
22 march 1915	Physical Drill & Coy Drill	

Instructions regarding War Diaries and Intelligence Summaries are contained in F. S. Regs., Part II. and the Staff Manual respectively. Title pages will be prepared in manuscript.

WAR DIARY
or
INTELLIGENCE SUMMARY.
(Erase heading not required.)

Army Form C. 2118.

Hour, Date, Place	Summary of Events and Information	Remarks and references to Appendices
23 March 1915.	Batt. worked on the road to Neuve Eglise. In the Evening the Batt marched via Neuve Eglise to Wolverghem and relieved the 5th K.O.S.L. Regt in trenches 8, 9 & 10a supporting no 4 / S.P. Souvenir Farm & St Quentin Cabaret No 2216 Pte Francis A Coy recd a G.S.W. in the left hip which penetrated into the abdomen, he was brought down & died shortly afterwards. He was buried in Wolverghem church yard. the burial service being read by M.O.	3 [illegible]
24 March 1915	Battalion in trenches as on night before - very quiet night 1774 Pte Coles D Coy slightly wounded in forehead while in a barn at Souvenir Farm about 3 p.m. 2145 Pte Arnold, later on was slightly wounded in the right thigh. Both men detained at Bde Hd Qrs.	
25 March	Batt in trenches - reliefs (inter Coy) were effected very quiet night.	

Instructions regarding War Diaries and Intelligence Summaries are contained in F. S. Regs., Part II. and the Staff Manual respectively. Title pages will be prepared in manuscript.

WAR DIARY
or
INTELLIGENCE SUMMARY.
(Erase heading not required.)

Army Form C. 2118.

Hour, Date, Place	Summary of Events and Information	Remarks and references to Appendices
26 March 1915	Batt in trenches trench 10 A was shelled by Enemy's Guns 679 Sergt Evans received serious shrapnel wounds and brought down same night – was conveyed to Neuve Eglise church and died same night. He was buried in the Village church yard. 1972 Pte Jackson 2165 Pte Scott recd rather serious shrapnell wounds and were conveyed to 1st Field Amb at the same time. 2171 Pte Pictor received fatal wounds from shrapnel & was buried in Wolverghem church yard. Burial service read by M. O.	3 [illegible]
27 March 1915	Batt in trenches 8 A trench was severely shelled by Enemy's guns during the morning and B. Coy suffered somewhat heavily. Great precision was made by enemy in searching trench & hedge to which the men were taken. Shells following them to each new spot it must be presumed that some good observation was being carried out. The following casualties occured 119 Pte Reynolds } killed outright shrapnel — All were buried in Wolverghem. Burial service being read by M. O. 1707 " Cook 1903 " Edwards	

(73989) W4141—463. 400,000. 9/14. H.&J.Ltd. Forms/C. 2118/10.

Instructions regarding War Diaries and Intelligence Summaries are contained in F. S. Regs., Part II. and the Staff Manual respectively. Title pages will be prepared in manuscript.

WAR DIARY
or
INTELLIGENCE SUMMARY.
(*Erase heading not required.*)

Army Form C. 2118.

Hour, Date, Place	Summary of Events and Information	Remarks and references to Appendices
27 March 1915 (Cont)	1398 Cl M Roberts received serious Shrapnel wounds 2223 " Mansel received " " " 1288 " Carey " " " " 1030 " Pearce " " " 2293 " L/Cpl Harris badly bruised in the shoulder and suffered from shock All these were transferred to 4 Field Amb. at Dranoutre Batt relieved at night by 5th K.O.R.L. Regt and marched back to Ravelsburgh where they were billetted as before.	3 men
28 March 1915	Batt rested in Billetts	
29 March 1915	8 Officers & 500 men proceeded to Wolverghem as working party at 5 p.m. and worked during the night under the direction of the R.E. The Brig. Gen. R Boyle visited Batt H^d Qrs and addressed all the Officers upon various details in trench work.	
30 March 1915	Steady Drill & inspection of arms under Coy arrangements.	

(73989) W4141—463. 400,000. 9/14. H.&J.Ltd. Forms/C. 2118/10.

Army Form C. 2118.

Instructions regarding War Diaries and Intelligence Summaries are contained in F. S. Regs., Part II. and the Staff Manual respectively. Title pages will be prepared in manuscript.

WAR DIARY
or
INTELLIGENCE SUMMARY.

(*Erase heading not required*.)

Hour, Date, Place	Summary of Events and Information	Remarks and references to Appendices
31 March 1915	The Batt relieved the 5th K.O.L.L. Regt in the trenches. Capt V E Ramsden 1/Batt S. W Borderers reported himself as Adjutant	3 mo

(73989) W4141—463. 400,000. 9/14. H.&J.Ltd. Forms/C. 2118/10.

SECOND BATTLE OF YPRES. April-May 1915.

History of the 3rd Monmouthshire Regiment.

3rd MONMOUTHSHIRE REGIMENT.

CHAPTER III - APPENDIX.

Mining operations at Hill 60. March - April.1915.

It will probably be of interest to follow the movements of the men of the Monmouthshire Regiment who left their Battalions in order to engage in mining work.

The General Staff had decided that mining on a much bigger scale than had ever before been undertaken in warfare was needed and accordingly the Battalion, whilst at Steenvoorde received orders to detail 1 Officer and 40 O.R. all of whom had to be experienced in mining to proceed to Ypres to engage in the work. A more suitable Battalion could not have been chosen to provide the men as the majority of the N.C.Os and men were miners in civil life.

On February 27th 1915 2/Lieutenant G.W.Lancaster, himself a Mining Engineer, together with 40 O.R. including Sgt Powles, Cpl. Hoare and L/Cpl. Leonard left Steenvoorde by Motor Bus for Ypres. Both Corporal Hoare and Lce-Corporal Leonard won the D.C.M. for their gallantry whilst engaged in this work. This party was given a hearty send off by the Battalion but their feeling of pride at being chosen for this very important work was tempered by regret at leaving the Battalion they loved so well.

They were accompanied by a similar party from the 1st Monmouthshire Regiment under Lieutenant Burnyeat, also a Mining Engineer. It is worthy of note that the two officers in charge of these parties bore names which have been long and honourably associated with the mining industry in South Wales and Monmouthshire.

On arrival at Ypres the Monmouths were attached to the Northumbrian Field Coy. R.E. (O/C Major Pollard D.S.O.) and were billeted in the Convent School in the Rue de Lille almost under the shadow of the old Cloth Hall. It is of pathetic interest to recall that on entering the school, the men found the scholars' books, papers and pens lying about the desks, evidence of their hurried departure when the Bombardment of the 1st Battle of Ypres commenced in the Autumn

/of

1914.

The men of the two Battalions at once became chums and during the whole time they were together the most harmonious relations prevailed, just as it did during the amalgamation of the three Battalions after their terrible experience in the second Battle of Ypres.

On St David's Day (March 1st) lieutenant Burnyeat took a party up to the front line in the St Eloi sector to commence the intended mining work, but this was found impossible owing to the heavy enemy shelling. On the following night another ineffectual attempt was made and again on March 3rd a party moved up under 2nd-Lieutenant Lancaster. On the way up Private Nat Lewis of Tredegar was hit in the leg, but pluckily carried on, although on arrival at the front line his boot was found to be full of blood. After having his wound dressed he was able to make his way back to a Field Ambulance.

The enemy continued a heavy bombardment of our trenches so 2nd-Lieutenant LANCASTER had no alternative but to withdraw his men. Whilst leading them back he was seriously wounded by a stray bullet and had to be carried to a Field Ambulance from which he was sent back to England.

The idea of mining at St Eloi was abandoned and the men had a few days rest in billets. About a week later a number of specially enlisted men from England joined the Company. They had been recruited by Lieut.-Colonel Norton Griffiths M.P. and had been engaged on the construction of the London Tube Railways, Sewers and work of that description. These men together with the Monmouths were formed into the 171st Tunnelling Company R.E., the first Company of this kind to be formed in France. It was then decided to start work on mining Hill 60 so called because the maps of the district showed that its summit was 60 metres above sea level. It could scarcely be dignified by the title of a hill but as the surrounding country was so flat its occupation by the enemy gave him a wonderful field of vision behind our lines and the purpose

of

of these operations was to dislodge him from this point of vantage. Our trenches lay at the foot of the hill with the enemy line roughly 120 yards away and above us. The hill was on the North side of the railway cutting and formed partly from the debris excavated from the cutting. This together with the clayey nature of the ground made tunnelling a difficult operation. It was estimated that saps driven from a point some few feet below our own line, with a rising gradient of about $\frac{1}{4}$" to the yard to allow for free drainage, would be about 30ft to 35 feet below the summit of the hill, a suitable depth for the charges.

Accordingly about the middle of March mining was started by the 171st Tunnelling Company R.E. under Colonel Jenorne C.B.,C.R.E. 28th Division with Major Griffiths in command of mining operations.

The French had already started a sap from an advanced piece of trench on the Southern face of the Hill and had driven it in some 20 yards before leaving it. This sap was very small in size- 3 feet x 2 feet - giving very little room for men to work, whilst all debris had to be placed in sandbags and dragged back by a rope. This made the rate of progression each day considerably less than that of the other saps, but owing to the fact that part of it was already driven and that the total drivage was less than the others it was the first sap to be finished and charged.

Those who knew that sap will remember that the body of a French Soldier had been built into the parapet by the mouth of the sap.

The two new saps were named M1 and M2, the French sap being called M3. M1 and M2 were started from small shafts 3 feet x 3 feet x 8 feet deep sunk in our front line. A small sump was made at the bottom of each shaft from which the water was bailed out by buckets. The saps were started and continued at a size 4 feet x $3\frac{1}{2}$ feet and were timbered throughout, this being made necessary by the soft nature of the ground. The work of excavating was done by two men at the face of each sap who placed each piece of debris carefully into a sandbag, this being done in order to comply

/with

with necessary precautions as to silence. The whole of these operations were carried on in almost uncanny silence and so successfully was it done that even when the powder chambers were being made right under their trenches the enemy were not aware of it. When the sandbags were filled they were placed on a small trolley run on wooden rails and pushed back to the shaft bottom where they were raised to the surface. The bags were stacked in the trench until night-time when they were used by the Infantry for repairing the trenches - any surplus being emptied behind the line in ground dead to view of the enemy.

The Miners did 24 hours at a time in the line, 2 hours in the sap and 4 hours out. During their 4 hours out they helped to dispose of the sandbags brought out from the sap, carried up material including the necessary timber which was already cut to the required size in order to obviate the noise of cutting timber in the sap.

The average rate of drivage in M1 and M2 was about 15 feet in 24 hours, although on one occasion one sap, manned entirely by Monmouthshire men, drove 16½ feet. This was the result of a test made by Lieutenant Burnyeat in order to prove that our men were as efficient miners as the specially enlisted men and on this occasion our men out drove the others by 2½ feet in 24 hours.

About the third week in March Lieutenant Burnyeat was wounded whilst leading his party back to Ypres and returned to England.

On March 24th Lieutenant W.P.Abbott (also a Mining Engineer) left the 3rd Monmouths and joined the mining party and remained with them until he contracted Enteric fever and was sent to hospital shortly before the Hill was blown up.

At that early stage of the war, trench maps were not as elaborate and accurate as they afterwards became, so that the only method of fixing the position of the enemy trenches was by use of aeroplane photographs. This was not as simple as it might appear owing to lens distortion, but that it was successful was proved by the demolition of the trenches when the mine was fired.

/the

The length of saps M1 and M2 was about 130 yards; and when driven to their full distance, cross headings were made to form the powder chambers - two to each sap - making a total of six chambers, each of which held one ton of explosive, in 100 lbs bags. The calculated amount required, as worked out by the formula used by the Engineers was three tons, but 100% was added to be on the safe side and to give Fritz a little bit extra for luck. The success of the explosion showed that the extra three tons was not wasted.

When the mines were charged, the detonators and cables fixed, the saps were each stemmed with three barriers of tightly rammed sandbags, each barrier 10 feet thick with an intervening air space of 10 feet.

All was now ready by the time appointed, in fact the mines were not fired for a few days after they were completed.

An R.E.Officer who did most excellent work on this job, Lieutenant Lionel Hill a South African Mining Engineer, who after Lieutenant Abbott had been sent to Hospital, looked after the Monmouthshire men as well, as though he was actually from Monmouthshire himself. He afterwards became a lieut.-Colonel and was in charge of the mining operations for one of our Armies.

The Hill was eventually blown up at 7.0. p.m. on April 17th just as the 3rd Battalion was marching out of Ypres to the front line with a result that is know to all - the required enemy trenches being completely obliterated, and quickly occupied by our troops with small loss.

After the blowing up of the Hill, the fury of the 2nd Battle of Ypres burst forth and the men of the 171st Company had some particularly tricky work to do especially counter-mining or "mole warfare" as it had been described. Counter-mining was always a most "windy" business as can be imagined for there was always present danger of the enemy having an advanced sap with a charge with a charge in it ready to explode when they thought our sap was near enough.

/It

It needs the pen of Edgar Allan Poe to conjure up the possibilities of the kind of warfare.

The 171st Company lost heavily in these counter-mining operations, many of the casualties being Monmouthshire men. At the end of May they were withdrawn from this sector and afterwards took part in other mining work, including the blowing up of the Wytschaete Ridge in 1917 under General Plumer.

When not engaged in offensive mining, were employed in making deep dugouts and similar work.

Although the Hill 60 mines were not on anything like as gigantic a scale as those at Wytschaete, La Boiselle and other mines in the later stages of the war, yet at the time they were greatly in advance of anything that had been attempted before and they paved the way for the greater development of mining warfare.

We can feel proud that those Monmouthshire men did their duty as nobly under the surface in the Salient as their old comrades did on the battlefield close by and that they too helped to add lustre to the name of the 1st and 3rd Battalions of the Monmouthshire Regiment.

83rd Bde.
28th Div.

Bde left 5th Div & rejoined 28th Div.6.4.15.

3rd M O N M O U T H S

A P R I L

1 9 1 5

April 1915

Instructions regarding War Diaries and Intelligence Summaries are contained in F. S. Regs., Part II. and the Staff Manual respectively. Title pages will be prepared in manuscript.

WAR DIARY
or
INTELLIGENCE SUMMARY.
(Erase heading not required.)

3rd Bn Monmouth Regt

Army Form C. 2118.

Hour, Date, Place	Summary of Events and Information	Remarks and references to Appendices
1st April 1915	A considerable amount of shelling on both sides	
2 April 1915	Pte Bullock A coy rec^d G S W jaw & shoulder. The Batt was relieved this night by 5/South Staffs during the relief a considerable amount of shelling by the Enemy occured. shells dropping on road around Wolverghem & St Quentin & towards Neuve Eglise. The Batt marched to Bailleul, where it was billetted. 2/Lt Crawford reported himself for Duty	
3 April 1915	The Batt rested. Lt E J O'Connor reported himself for duty	
4 April 1915	Batt attended Divine Service in Caisse D'Epargne rue de Poisson Bailleul	
5 April 1915	The Batt proceeded by march route to billets 2½ miles N W of Wanticle [illegible]	

(73989) W4141—463. 400,000. 9/14. H.&J.Ltd. Forms/C. 2118/10.

Instructions regarding War Diaries and Intelligence Summaries are contained in F. S. Regs., Part II. and the Staff Manual respectively. Title pages will be prepared in manuscript.

WAR DIARY
or
INTELLIGENCE SUMMARY.
(Erase heading not required.)

Army Form C. 2118.

Hour, Date, Place	Summary of Events and Information	Remarks and references to Appendices
6 April 1915	Coy Bombs Machine Gun Officer Adj. proceeded by motor Bus to the trenches East of Ypres for observation purposes & instructions from the French troops occupying the same, staying there for 24 hours.	
7 April 1915	Inspection of the whole Brigade by General Sir Horace Smith Dorrien G.C.B. etc. and an address by him to the Officers & representatives N.C.Os.	
8 April 1915	Batt proceeded by motor Bus to Ypres and from there to the Zonnebeke Sector where it relieved the 2nd Batt 146 Regiment (French).	
9 April 1915	B Coy suffered a good deal from bomb-throwing by the enemy 2087 Pte Apsley fatally wounded buried in wood at Zonnebeke 2251 Pte Gillard G.S.W. right thigh & left forefinger - transferred to 83rd Fld Amb. 2151 Pte Wilkes G.S.W. forehead slight trans 83 Fld Amb. 6th 1043 Pte Rodgers G.S.W. forefinger left hand Trans 83 F.A. 1801 L/C. Place G.S.W. Head & left Shoulder - slight 1314 Pte Watkins G.S.W. Rt Shin slight [illegible]	

(73989) W4141—463. 400,000. 9/14. H.&J.Ltd. Forms/C. 2118/10.

Instructions regarding War Diaries and Intelligence Summaries are contained in F. S. Regs., Part II. and the Staff Manual respectively. Title pages will be prepared in manuscript.

WAR DIARY
or
INTELLIGENCE SUMMARY.
(Erase heading not required.)

Army Form C. 2118.

Hour, Date, Place	Summary of Events and Information	Remarks and references to Appendices
9 April 1915	2149 Pte E Purcell Rt thigh kept at Hd Qrs	
	2110 " J Denford G.S.W. Foot slight kept at Hd Qrs	
	2183 " Bishop G.S.W. back slight kept at Hd Qrs	
	2370 " J Llewellyn G.S.W. Head slight	
	B Coy suffered slightly from Shrapnel in left trench	
	16 Sergt Jones G.S.W. hip slight wounded on 9th did not report to M.O. until 10.	
	2236 J Marshall (MG) G.S.W in Abdomen fatal Buried by C.O in wood of Zonnebeke	
	1721 Pte Warner G.S.W Left ankle trans 83 F A	
	1483 Pte Matthews G S W Abdomen fatal buried by C O Wood of Zonnebeke	
	C Coy 493 Sgt A T Hatfield G S W Abdomen being serious sent to 83 Fd Ambce	
10 April 1915	Both trenches suffered slightly from Shrapnel and a good deal of parapets of both was blown down	
	D Coy 2361 Pte Powell G.S.W. Left thigh sent to 83 F A	
	511 L/Cpl Hawes G.S.W Left shoulder	
	2381 Pte J Snow G.S.W heart fatal buried in Zonnebeke by M.O.	

Instructions regarding War Diaries and Intelligence Summaries are contained in F. S. Regs., Part II. and the Staff Manual respectively. Title pages will be prepared in manuscript.

WAR DIARY
or
INTELLIGENCE SUMMARY.
(*Erase heading not required.*)

Army Form C. 2118.

Hour, Date, Place	Summary of Events and Information	Remarks and references to Appendices
10. April 1915 Contd	C. Coy. 2305 Pte Steen G.S.W. Forehead. Repeat 2nd B. Coy. 1702 " Gallagher G.S.W. right cheek Sent to 83. F.A 1821. Cpl Hawkins accidental G.S.W. Left hand sent to 83. F.A.	
11. April 1915	A hostile Aeroplane passed over Hd Qrs Dugout and dressing station dropping two bombs neither of which exploded St. Sergt Hailstone C Coy had both his feet blown off whilst in the trenches. He had his feet amputated by Bn M.O. and was transfered to 83 F.A He died next morning & was buried at Potize E of Ypres by the Chaplain. 2210 Pte J Baines received G.S.W in head - Fatal - was buried in wood by M.O.	
12 April 1915	1796 Pte Waggett accidentally by his own rifle in left hand sent to 83. F.A. The Battalion was relieved by the 5th K.O. Regt and marched back to Ypres where it was billeted in midtown	
13 April 1915	Battalion rested.	

Instructions regarding War Diaries and Intelligence Summaries are contained in F. S. Regs., Part II. and the Staff Manual respectively. Title pages will be prepared in manuscript.

WAR DIARY
or
INTELLIGENCE SUMMARY.
(*Erase heading not required.*)

Army Form C. 2118.

Hour, Date, Place	Summary of Events and Information	Remarks and references to Appendices
14 Feb 1915 April?	Batt rested. Capt Lancaster & 3 men proceeded to trenches to report upon suspected sniping by enemy reported nothing proceeding	
15 Feb 1915 "	Batt rest moved in the evening from the billetts near town & took over billets in Lunatic Asylum NE of town f. R E F Regt	
16. Feb 1915. "	Battallion rested	
17 Feb 1915 "	Batt rested and proceeded to the trenches in the evening taking over from the 5th K.O. Regt 1820 L/C Hawkins C Coy G S W forearm slight sent to 83 FA	
18 Feb 1915 "	Batt in trenches. B Coy in right trench D in left Trenches bombed by trench mortars a good deal. Pte E Butler. B. Co. G S W head sent to 83 FA 1526. Pte Bishop B Coy fatally wounded in head Buried by C O in wood at Zonnebeke 1618 Pte Davies seriously wounded in temple sent to FA.	

(73989) W4141—463. 400,000. 9/14. H.&J.Ltd. Forms/C. 2118/10.

Instructions regarding War Diaries and Intelligence Summaries are contained in F. S. Regs., Part II. and the Staff Manual respectively. Title pages will be prepared in manuscript.

WAR DIARY
or
INTELLIGENCE SUMMARY.
(*Erase heading not required.*)

Army Form C. 2118.

Hour, Date, Place	Summary of Events and Information	Remarks and references to Appendices
18 April 1915 (Continued)	2144 Pte Dovey slightly wounded in scalp sent to 83 F.A 1134 " Barrell " " " " " 2451 " Danford " " " " [illegible]	
19 April 1915	1031. Pte D J Pritchard slightly wounded 4 SW forearm sent to 83 FA 121. Pte L Coleman (SB) 4 SW right shoulder slight " " 2458 " W Davies (SB) 4 SW " arm " "	
20 April 1915	39 Sergt Wellington C Coy 4 SW head. Dangerous sent to 83 F.A 1063 Pte A. Dimmerick D Coy 4 SW head, dangerous sent to 83 F.A	
21 April 1915	920 Sgt Farmer 4 SW in Abdomen sent to 83 F.A Lt J Worton slightly in neck " " " L/C S Reed 4 SW in right cheek slight returned to duty same day 2134 Pte Llewellyn slightly wounded in neck returned to duty same day 1959 Pte M O'Hearn C Coy slight 4 SW left thigh sent to 83 F.A	

(73989) W4141—463. 400,000. 9/14. H.&J.Ltd. Forms/C. 2118/10.

Instructions regarding War Diaries and Intelligence Summaries are contained in F. S. Regs., Part II. and the Staff Manual respectively. Title pages will be prepared in manuscript.

WAR DIARY
or
INTELLIGENCE SUMMARY.
(Erase heading not required.)

Army Form C. 2118.

Hour, Date, Place	Summary of Events and Information	Remarks and references to Appendices
22 April 1915	Inter relief of Coys was carried out A Coy to right fire trench - C Co left 2300 Pte J Heaton. C Coy slightly wounded in scalp sent to 83 F A 2313 Pte J Jones C Coy slightly wounded in left upper arm sent to 83 F A 1487 L/Cpl Watkins C Coy fatally wounded G S W - dead. Buried in Zonnebeke wood by C O 2152 Pte Prescott B Coy seriously wounded G S W in right thigh sent to 83 F A 2153 Pte G H Bishop B Coy fatally wounded in abdomen buried by C. O in Wood at Zonnebeke Pte Rushgrove D Coy G S W sent to Suffolk Dressing Station 2255 Pte Leanshall A Co accidentally wounded by G S W in foot sent to 83 F A. 1126 Pte J Jones B Coy G S W in right hip slightly sent to 83 F A.	

(73989) W4141—463. 400,000. 9/14. H.&J.Ltd. Forms/C. 2118/10.

Instructions regarding War Diaries and Intelligence Summaries are contained in F. S. Regs., Part II. and the Staff Manual respectively. Title pages will be prepared in manuscript.

WAR DIARY
or
INTELLIGENCE SUMMARY.
(Erase heading not required.)

Army Form C. 2118.

Hour, Date, Place	Summary of Events and Information	Remarks and references to Appendices
23 April 1915	695 Pte Rendall C Coy G.S.W. in left forearm Sent to 83 F.A	
	2493 " Webber slightly wounded in 3 left finger kept at H^d Qrs	
	2582 Pte J Baker G.S.W. in right arm slight Sent to 83 F.A	
	2016 L/C Clifford A Coy G.S.W. in right arm " " "	
	2430 Pte Armstrong slightly wounded in scalp " " "	
	1505 Pte Walters (S.B) seriously " in left side " "	
	1973 Pte F. Jenkins C Coy G.S.W. in cheek superficial " "	
24 April 1915	Pte J. Jones B Coy G.S.W. in left shoulder " " "	
	2477 Pte Bowden A Coy G.S.W. in head fatal buried in wood at Zonnebeke	
	Battalion first fatal casualties of Officers occurred Lt Onions was fatally wounded in the head whilst conducting a party back to dugouts. Died as soon as he was conveyed to 83 F.A.	
25 April 1915	Inter Coy change carried out D Coy to left trench & B Coy to right trench	
	1777 Pte Collier D Coy G.S.W. left shoulder slight	
	1441 " C.O. Williams A Coy G.S.W. 3rd left toe sent to 83 F.A	
	31 Pte Meredith accidently blew off tip of right forefinger	

(73989) W4141—463. 400,000. 9/14. H.&J.Ltd. Forms/C. 2118/10.

Instructions regarding War Diaries and Intelligence Summaries are contained in F. S. Regs., Part II. and the Staff Manual respectively. Title pages will be prepared in manuscript.

WAR DIARY
or
INTELLIGENCE SUMMARY.
(Erase heading not required.)

Army Form C. 2118.

Hour, Date, Place	Summary of Events and Information	Remarks and references to Appendices
26 April 1915.	1810. Pte Watkins B Coy 2318 Pte A Harris (S.B.) 2319 Pte Hancock (S.B.) were all slightly wounded while carrying down 1801 L/C F. Pearce who had been seriously wounded in the left side & chest. He was also wounded again while being on the stretcher - slightly in the right leg. These wounds were effected by a shrapnel shell.	
	2122 Pte Baggott 4 S.W. in right arm Sent to 83 F A	
	2029 Pte Watkins D Coy slightly in head " " "	
	516. Sergt G Jones seriously wounded in head "	
	1683 Pte Rees slightly wounded in head	
	1231 L/C Thomas D Coy slightly wounded in head " " "	
	553 Pte Jones seriously wounded lower jaw 4 S.W. " " "	
	1138. " Jones D Coy slightly wounded in throat " " "	
	In the latter part of this day the trench occupied by D Coy was bombed by trench mortars [& the following casualties occurred	
	638 Pte G Evans 331 Pte W Bevans 2003 Pte Arnold three fatal wounds and buried at Zonnebeke	
	802. Pte Evans wound in head dangerous Sent to 83 F A	
	Pte D Edwards slightly wounded in right thigh Sent to 83rd F A.	

(73989) W4141—463. 400,000. 9/14. H.&J.Ltd. Forms/C. 2118/10.

Instructions regarding War Diaries and Intelligence Summaries are contained in F. S. Regs., Part II. and the Staff Manual respectively. Title pages will be prepared in manuscript.

WAR DIARY
or
INTELLIGENCE SUMMARY.
(*Erase heading not required.*)

Army Form C. 2118.

Hour, Date, Place	Summary of Events and Information	Remarks and references to Appendices
26 April 1915. Contd.	1313 Pte A T. Watkins B. Coy was fatally wounded in head 2153 Pte W Roach also fatally wounded in head, both of these were buried at Zonnebeke by C.O. together with the above of D Co 1876. Pte J. E. Overton D Co slightly wounded in right knee. Kept at Hd Qrs 1548. Pte J. Phillips G S W. slight at Hd Qrs	
27. April 1915.	In connection with the operations going on around Ypres the following message from the C in chief was received from Brigade. "The C in C wishes to express to all ranks of the 27 Div his appreciation for the manner in which the 28 Divn has borne itself under the strain of the last few days - He feels confident that they will stubbornly hold their ground for the short time the call is made of them. The Corps Comdr wishes to endorse the remarks of the C in C Major General Bulfin congratulates the 28 Div on the well merited praise.	

(73989) W4141—463. 400,000. 9/14. H.&J.Ltd. Forms/C. 2118/10.

Army Form C. 2118.

WAR DIARY
or
INTELLIGENCE SUMMARY.
(*Erase heading not required.*)

Instructions regarding War Diaries and Intelligence Summaries are contained in F. S. Regs., Part II. and the Staff Manual respectively. Title pages will be prepared in manuscript.

Hour, Date, Place	Summary of Events and Information	Remarks and references to Appendices
28 April 1915	A further congratulatory message was received from the G.O.C. 28th Div. as follows. "The G.O.C. 28th Div wishes it to be made known to all ranks that their efforts during the past few days whilst fighting on the northern Front, & during tours of duty in our original trenches are fully appreciated by those in command. The Army Corps Commander considers that the conduct of the troops of the 28th Divn has been beyond praise".	
29. April 1915.	Very quiet day.	

(73989) W4141—463. 400,000. 9/14. H.&J.Ltd. Forms/C. 2118/10.

CHAPTER III.

SECOND BATTLE OF YPRES - APRIL - MAY 1915.

1. Battle of Gravenstafel April 22nd - 23rd.
2. Battle of St. Julien April 24th - May 4th.
3. Battle of Frezenberg May 8th - 13th.
4. Battle of Bellewaarde May 24th - 25th.

DIVISIONS engaged April 22nd - May 25th :-

1st Canadian.

28th, 27th, 5th, 4th, 50th, Lahore.

1st, 2nd and 3rd Cavalry Divisions.

Killed, wounded & missing - 2,091 Officers. 58,169 Other ranks.

The Battalion left billets at Boeschepe on April 8th and proceeded by bus to Ypres. It was dark when we reached the Grande Place. The Cloth Hall and St. Martin's Cathedral were wrapped in a mysterious gloom. We were conscious of a wide space, filled with moving bodies of troops, but unable to discern anything clearly. But it was not the time for such reflections. The order was to draw rations and go to the trenches, so the Battalion moved off through the Menin Gate, up the Zonnebeke Road to Frezenberg, and then struck off half right across country to the Polygon Wood in the South-east of the Salient.

Battalion Headquarters were in dugouts in the mound known as the Butte de Polygon, now surmounted by an Australian War Memorial. close to the 'Squeaking Pump' which was reputed to have founded the fame of that officer artist who created that delightful character "Old Bill", and did much by his quaint humour to lighten our darkest hours. Two companies were in the front line, one in support in dugouts in the wood, and one behind the wood. The Polygon Wood at this time was still little damaged, a wood chiefly of pines in a light soil with bare patches of sand at intervals: now every big tree is down and a thick undergrowth has entirely altered the landscape. The dugouts were of French construction, not excavated many inches deep and so affording little protection either from rifle fire or from weather, but roofed with green pine needles and irregularly placed, so that they were well hidden from the air: this was very necessary as enemy aircraft were quite active. The French had made rather an artistic job of them and had written verses on the trees, while one romantic Poilu had named his dwelling "Villa ma Rose".

The Wood was not a 'wholesome' place. It was exposed to fire both from south and east, with a chance of a bullet dropping from the north: fortunately the contour made some of the ground 'dead'. One feature of life in the wood was a fair sized German fieldgun which precisely at the quarter to every hour in the twenty-four fired one shell in the direction of Battalion H.Q. The shell fell with a crash among the trees, but never damaged anything else.

The trenches lay east and south-east of the wood, opposite Reutel and Becelaere, and followed a most irregular line. The right half was split up into four sections, each holding a platoon, but not continuous and the left company was separated from the right by a long piece of trench, called No Man's Land, which was only held at night by a platoon from the supports in the wood. The parapets were bad, the dugouts and traverses were few, and there was nothing in front but some coils of "piano" wire. The enemy was 200 yards away on the right, but on the extreme left within bombing distance. The right trench had been called Pall Mall and the left Whitehall, but these names never 'caught on' among us. On April 8th "B" company took the right hand trench and "D" the left, with "A" and "C" in support. We took over from the 2nd Battalion of the 146th Regiment of the French Army, who departed in their own casual way. One of their platoon Commanders raised a smile on the face of his opposite number by giving him a little trench map, whereon the only dugout was marked "Your Home" and then hurrying away after his men.

Morning gave an opportunity to view the situation. The French, it appeared, had not done much work on the parapets which were by no means bullet proof, and a great deal of time had to be put in each night in strengthening the front line defences. They had also not been active in harassing the enemy, who were discovered our first morning to be cooking their breakfasts in braziers on the top of the parapet ! An intimation that this must cease was of course sent over, but this provoked a reply of rifle grenades and the nasty little whizzbang that makes no noise till it hits the parapet. They had bigger guns too that knocked our trenches about, and one day a hostile aeroplane dropped bombs at Battalion H.Q. In the first few days the French Artillery was behind us and we had our first experience of the famous "75's" but our own artillery when it arrived was not numerous and very short of ammunition.

It was a quiet period for the Salient, but it was clear from the first that it was a hotter place than Wulverghem, and casualties were more frequent.

On April 10th there was an inter-company relief and as usual the line was voted better than support.

On the 12th the 5th King's Own relieved us and we went to billets in Ypres. There was now an opportunity to examine this famous old city by daylight. It was seriously damaged and there was occasional shelling, but the bulk of the Cloth Hall still stood and was not much more ruinous than it appears in the photographs taken in November 1914. The civil population had by no means all left. Cafes did a good trade and shops were selling not only wine and cigars, but such useful articles for the trenches as refills for electric torches and solidified fuel. British troops abounded and no doubt their presence was known to the enemy though no one was supposed to go out till after dark. It was a curious interlude in a strenuous life. One scene comes back to memory, a boxing competition between two companies in a school playground with a British band playing and overhead a German Taube !

On the 15th the Battalion moved into the Lunatic Asylum near the Dixmude Gate and on the 17th returned to the trenches. This was the beginning of great events, for this evening Hill 60 was blown up and captured by the 13th Brigade. Parties from the 1st and 3rd Monmouthshire Battalions who formed the 171st Tunnelling Company with expert tunnel navvies sent out specially from a firm of London Contractors, had been engaged in preparing for this event and had won by their success distinction as expert workers underground. Lt. G.W. Lancaster who commanded the first party from the Thirds had been badly wounded in this work and was succeeded by 2/Lt. W.P. Abbott. The British guns were going hard on both sides of the road as the Battalion marched out, and it was a relief to reach Frezenberg and go across country before the Germans replied by shelling the roads: the Staff had calculated correctly and got the Battalion off the road in time.

On arriving in the trenches the Battalion found things much as before, and carried on with the usual routine, though there was a feeling of uncertainty in the air. One obvious sign of trouble was that no relief arrived at the usual time. Companies relieved each other and relieved again, but the 5th King's Own never again appeared and gradually news came of what was happening near enough, but yet so far off that we learned of it first from the English papers. The enemy clearly was stirring and April 22nd saw the opening of a heavy bombardment a few miles to our north. They had shelled our billets in the Lunatic Asylum and destroyed not a battalion but some officer's kits, so ran one rumour. The truth was that the kits were buried by the shelling, and later dug out by a fatigue party under the Sergeant-Drummer ! Then came authentic news of the first gas attack on April 22nd, the retreat of the French on the north of the Salient, the magnificent resistance of the Canadians, the advance of the enemy towards Ypres and the repeated British counter-attacks which held up the advance and recovered some of the lost ground.

On the night of April 24th "D" Company was employed with two companies of the 1st K.O.Y.L.I., and 2nd King's Own in digging a new line for the Canadians after the counter-attack, but otherwise the Battalion had only to stand by in the Polygon Line, and April 29th is noted in the War Diary as a "very quiet day". At the same time casualties occurred day after day. On April 24th 2/Lt. Wilfred Onions, the son of the well-known Miners Leader (the late Mr. Alfred Onions, M.P) was fatally wounded as he was marching a party back to the dugouts behind the Polygon Wood - the first fatal casualty among officers - and on May 1st Lt. Martin, the M.G. officer was killed. He was a great loss: he was an officer greatly beloved by his own men - "My people" as he always called them - and a keen machine gunner. He had made a name for himself before the War in the world of science and applied himself with characteristic thoroughness to the study of his favourite weapon. On the morning of May 3rd Lt. Crawford was seriously wounded in the head whilst firing over the parapet, the bullet striking the foresight of his rifle. Lts. Reed and Worton were also slightly wounded.

The general situation was worse than we knew. The gas

attack had broken the line in the north of the Salient and enabled the Germans to bring their guns up on the Pilckem Ridge and adjoining high ground and enfilade the area held by the British which was barely 6,000 yards wide by 9,000 yards deep. Of this area the Polygon Wood was the most easterly outpost. Such a position was clearly untenable both from an Infantry and an Artillery point of view and was rapidly developing into a bottle shaped zone, which must have inevitably been pinched off at the neck with disastrous results. To avoid this danger and shorten the line, the G.O.C.-in-C ordered a withdrawal to a line approximately just east of Hooge Chateau and Frezenberg, south of St. Julien and converging on the Yser Canal near Boesinghe. This had the effect of shortening the front line by 5,000 yards.

The movement was commenced on the night of May 1st by bringing back the guns to new positions and evacuating dumps. The occupation of the new front line by the supporting troops and the evacuation of the Polygon Wood was effected on the night of May 3rd. This operation on the 83rd Brigade front began by withdrawing at 9.30 p.m., two companies each of the 2nd King's Own, 3rd Monmouths (B & D Coys.) and 1st K.O.Y.L.I. These companies were ordered to fall back as far as the new line, and stand fast there until the safe withdrawal of the other two companies of each Battalion was assured. The latter withdrew at 10.30 p.m., and in order to conceal the movement from the enemy, each of these companies were ordered to leave behind a covering party of one officer and 20 O.R's to fire occasional shots and send up Verey Lights from various points in the trenches and finally fall back on the main body at midnight. The 3rd Monmouth covering parties were commanded by Lt. Reed (A. Coy.) and Lt. Bennett (C. Coy.) who carried out their difficult duties with complete success.

The whole operation was under the control of officers posted by the Brigade at the N.W. corner of the Wood, in telephone communication with Brigade H.Q. and they withdrew after all troops were clear. Amongst the officers detailed for this duty was Lt. H.A. Hodges ("D" Coy). In the retirement all ammunition and a considerable quantity of trench stores were brought back. As an indication of the success of the movement the enemy were still firing on our empty trenches at 5 a.m.

In the meantime the three battalions fell back along the railway, the 2nd King's Own and 1st K.O.Y.L.I. being withdrawn to huts west of Ypres, whilst the 3rd Monmouths turned off the railway to Verlorenhoek and followed the main road down to G.H.Q. line at Potijze.

The trenches in the G.H.Q. line ran across the main road just east of Potijze Chateau, which was on the north side. Battalion H.Q. was at Lancer Farm south of the road. May 4th was spent here, a dull, detestable day, with nothing to do and not much to eat, and heavy shells flying overhead into Ypres.

About 6 a.m. the enemy sent forward their first patrols and at 10 a.m. began bombarding the new front line, which they had registered some days earlier during construction. At 10.30 a.m. they were observed digging in at distances 400/700 yards away. At 5 p.m. the front line trenches on the north and centre of the 83rd Brigade front were reported as seriously damaged.

The evening of May 4th saw the beginning of the Battalion's hardest trial and greatest achievement. The strain and stress was all over within a week, but during that period the 3rd Monmouths were involved in some of the hardest fighting of the War, suffered heavy casualties, and though outnumbered by the enemy and without adequate artillery support, held up the German attack at a crucial point of the line.

On this evening "A" Coy. (Capt. Baker) and "C" Coy. (Capt. Steel) moved up in/to support trenches and dugouts north of the road at the western foot of the Frezenberg Ridge; "B" Coy. (Capt. Gattie) went up to reinforce the 1st York & Lancs on the right of the Brigade and "D" Coy. (Major Lewis) remained in reserve at Potijze.

The new front line which had been hastily and poorly constructed suffered severely from the bombardment. So bad did conditions become that both the 2nd East Yorks and 5th King's Own were compelled that night to dig a new line just behind the original one. Casualties had been heavy and the wounded were removed with great difficulty during the night whilst the dead had to be buried where they fell.

May 5th opened with a still severer bombardment, and the front line troops were reported as being in a very exhausted condition. Quite early in the morning "C" Company was called upon to reinforce the 2nd East Yorks on the south of the road. Their C.O., Lt.-Col. Pike, came up to show the way and guided by him the company crossed the road and made diagonally up the ridge between Wilde Wood and Wilde Cottage to the edge of the railway. At this point Capt. Steel decided to advance with half the company north-east straight over the ridge. In the meantime he sent word down to Capt. Gorman, his second in command, to carry out the reinforcement with the other half company.

As Capt. Steel topped the ridge, he and his party came under full observation and lost heavily from machine-gun fire, and it was a marvel how anyone reached the front line. The success of the reinforcement was due to the gallant and unhesitating leadership of Capt. Steel. Further he brought his medical knowledge into splendid use and attended to the wounded, regardless of all danger. For these fine services he was awarded the Military Cross, the first officer of the Battalion to receive this honour. In the meantime Capt.

Gorman arrived at the head of the second Half of the company, who were lying on the edge of the railway cutting. As casualties had been heavy, it was difficult to ascertain orders or ~~to~~ get into communication with the first half which had disappeared over the ridge. Capt. Gorman decided to follow the railway, and on reaching the Frezenberg Level Crossing, he found the front line trench just over the crest of the ridge. This he reconnoitred under heavy shell fire for 80 yards without finding a living soul. The trenches, being on a forward slope and following a hedge and treeline, were an easy mark for the enemy artillery who had the position absolutely taped and made it quite untenable. On leaving the trench to rejoin his men, Capt. Gorman was caught by a machine gun and fell wounded into the railway cutting, being hit in no less than eight places. His servant, Pte. Gray. pluckily remained with him for a considerable time in a very exposed situation till ordered back. A few minutes after Capt. Gorman was hit, Lt. Bennett was wounded getting out of the same trench. Realizing the impossibility of holding this trench, which was practically obliterated and completely exposed to machine-gun fire, Capt. Gorman gave orders for his men to reform behind the ridge. It was then that C.S.M. Gravenor attempted to carry out the reinforcement in a southerly direction across the level crossing to the front line held by the 1st York & Lancs which lay 150 yards beyond. He was almost immediately wounded, but continued to encourage his men on, and for this gallant action he was awarded the D.C.M. and the Croix de Guerre avec Palmes.

The hostile machine-gunners in Rabbit Villa were now fully aware that a force was trying to advance by the level crossing and kept up such a hot fire that the remainder of the second half of "C" company were driven back to dig in in Wilde Wood just in their rear. Later in the day the survivors managed to work their way forward to a line of dugouts behind Frezenberg. "C" Coy. in the front line was relieved that night and Captain Steel was able to get his company together again in the support line behind Frezenberg. For the next three nights "C" Coy. was busily engaged with their much depleted strength in carrying rations and ammunition to the other three companies in the front line, and Capt. Steel personally took up rations to the hard-pressed machine-gunners who were attached to his company.

"A" Coy. was in support of the 5th King's Own and in advance of that battalion's reserve company. On the morning of the 5th, an hour after "C" Coy's advance, the 5th King's Own asked for reinforcements. It was arranged to reinforce by platoons and Capt. R.A. Lewis started off with No. 1. Our artillery support was inadequate, the ground sloped downwards towards the fire trench and the only communication trench was bad and finished altogether before it reached the front line. As soon as Capt. Lewis appeared over the ridge, his party came under artillery and machine-gun fire and suffered severely. Finally Capt. Lewis was badly hit by a machine-gun. He managed to crawl into a hole with a few men, including Pte. Skidmore, who was awarded the D.C.M. for bandaging Pte. Roach's wound under very heavy fire, and then attempting to get back with information. The experience of these two companies showed that any reinforcement by daylight must be very costly, as there were no proper communication trenches and the advance had to take place across the open on a forward slope with very little support from our artillery. After dark for these few nights it was curiously quiet for the enemy was probably too busy consolidating to give trouble.

"D" Coy. (Major W.A.Lewis) remained in reserve in the G.H.Q. line during May 5th. Shelling had been severe and Lt. Hodges and several men were wounded. That night it moved up with "A" Coy. to relieve the East Yorks and the reinforcements they had received during the day from "C" Coy.

The East Yorks had suffered very severely during that day and one company had only 20 effectives left. "A" and "D" companies occupied the front line from the Zonnebeke Road south to the railway, with a few of "A" Coy. on the north of the road in touch with the 2nd King's Own who had the same night relieved the 5th King's Own. The Machine Gun Section were called upon the same evening to relieve the East Yorks machine-gunners whose guns had been knocked out. One gun was placed just south of the road, where it commanded a fine field of fire and the main road, and the other on the right of "D" Coy. commanded the railway. Communication was kept up across the road by throwing messages in empty jam tins. The same evening Battalion H.Q. moved up to dugouts on the west of Frezenberg, about 100 yards in rear of "C" Coy.

The heavy shelling ceased at night-fall and enabled the reliefs to be carried out.

During this night and the following night the 1st K.O.Y.L.I were engaged full strength in digging shelter trenches against shell fire at various points just behind the front line. Much of this work was abortive as these narrow trenches would not remain open for long without revetment which was not available.

Next day, May 6th, there was shelling, but less severe than on the 5th, and no attempt at an attack by the enemy. They were no doubt bringing up their artillery in the attempt to push through to the Channel Ports. There was only a thinly held line to bar their way, but happily it stood.

May 7th opened with a heavier bombardment which caused many casualties. In "A" coy 2/Lt. Sorby was so severely wounded that he died the same night. In the evening Lt. Worton, who had only returned from hospital the same day, was killed while taking up a party of "C" coy. to the front line. "D" Coy. lost 2/Lt. Townsend - killed - whilst its commander, Major Lewis was wounded.

So dawned the most critical day of the great battle, the 8th of May. The 3rd Monmouths lay astride the Zonnebeke Road, the apex of the Salient, two companies in the front line with one in support and the fourth company not far away to the south. Half a mile to the north was their sister battalion the 1st Monmouthshires in the 84th Brigade. Holding the position with them were their comrades of the 83rd Brigade, the 2nd King's Own to the north and to the south the 1st K.O.Y.L.I. who relieved the 1st York & Lancs and "B" Coy. 3rd Monmouths on the night of May 7th. The Brigade had been in the line without relief since April 17th. Its numbers were greatly reduced, and the artillery behind were few in numbers and woefully short of ammunition. As indicating the desperate position of the British troops in respect to artillery support, it is now authoritatively stated that the heavy British guns during this period of the 2nd Battle of Ypres were limited to :-

One 9.2-inch howitzer;
Eight 60-pdrs.;
Four old 6-inch howitzers;
Twelve obsolete 4.7-inch guns.

Against them the Germans brought up at least 260 heavy guns and howitzers.

There was nothing except the Division between the enemy and Ypres on that day and they got as far as Verlorenhoek, but the British soldier proverbially does not know when he is beaten and the Germans were kept back somehow till fresh troops were brought up in the evening to fill the many gaps. The enemy on their side were "all out" to push through. They had guns on the high ground enfilading the British position and smothering our artillery, they had field guns well forward, they had innumerable machine-guns, and six Divisions of their best and freshest troops, against the depleted ranks of the war-worn and weary 27th and 28th Divisions. Their bombardment opened up at 5.30 a.m. and the trenches lying on the forward slope were badly damaged and almost untenable.

during the last terrible days and with him had often helped to stiffen the defence by cheery encouragement. He now refused to be carried back and was soon taken prisoner. His wounds were of such a nature that he was one of the first prisoners of war to be exchanged, but unhappily he died much regretted before the end of the War. He was a fine type of Regular soldier from whom all ranks learnt much.

After hanging on to this position for some time and holding up the advance, orders came about 11 a.m., from the Brigade to retire on the G.H.Q. line near Potijze.

Lt. McLean, M.O., 3rd Monmouths and Lt. Marriott, M.O., 1st Monmouths had established a Dressing Station just east of Verlorenhoek: at 11 a.m., they received orders to retire their detachments, but after sending back the stretcher-bearers they found a number of wounded still coming back and so decided to carry on, till the enemy were practically in the village and Lt. McLean was wounded.

Just before mid-day the 2nd East Yorks were ordered to counter-attack and after reaching Verlorenhoek with heavy casualties had to fall back on the G.H.Q. line.

At 2.30 p.m. 1st York & Lancs. and 3rd Middlesex counter-attacked north and south of the railway, remnants of the 2nd East Yorks, 1st K.O.Y.L.I., 2nd King's Own, 3rd Monmouths, 5th King's Own going up into support. In this action Lord Richard Cavendish, C.O., 5th King's Own was wounded.

At 3.30 p.m. 2nd East Surreys, 3rd Royal Fusiliers arrived and were sent up in support. The counter-attack, practically unsupported by artillery, made slow progress and by 5.30 p.m. was held up at a line running from Verlorenhoek south over the railway. This line was consolidated with fresh troops during the night and eventually became the approximate position of the front line until the British advance in 1917.

In the meantime the Battalion with the exception of "B" Coy. was withdrawn and marched back to the huts at Vlamertinghe.

"B" Coy. throughout the battle was separated from the rest of the Battalion. On May 4th it reinforced 1st York & Lancs, coming under the orders of the C.O. of that battalion, and took over a trench on the extreme right of the Brigade and Division from a company of the K.R.R.C. 27th Division. The next unit on the right was "Princess Pats". The position was in front of the Wood near Red Lodge, about 300yards south of the Roulers railway. The trench was newly dug like the rest of the line and not deep. It was also on a forward slope and the only communication trench was full of mud and impassable. Further it lay along a lane with a hedge on one side and a line of poplars on the other, so that it was an admirable mark for the enemy's artillery observing on the Westhoek Ridge. On May 5th and in a smaller degree on May 6th and 7th the enemy bombarded the trench, but it was so narrow and well traversed that the damage was comparatively slight and casualties not as heavy as might be expected after such a bombardment. Sergt. Nash, a Territorial with much service, was killed on the 6th. It was peculiarly noticeable here that the nights were absolutely quiet and it was safe to walk about in the open behind the front line. Rations and letters came up regularly and one fortunate officer even received a tin of cooked sausages. On the night of May 7th the company was relieved by a company of the 1st K.O.Y.L.I. under Capt. Mallinson[x] and "B" Coy. went into support in the wood just behind the line, which was adorned with French dugouts like those in the Polygon Wood.

---

[x] The remainder of the 1st K.O.Y.L.I. held the line as far north as the Roulers railway.

At daybreak on May 8th "B" Coy came in for the shelling which the enemy poured on the whole line. They were evidently searching for a battery behind the wood, but did not neglect the wood, itself and killed two officers, Lt. Groves and 2/Lt. Palmer, in one dugout. Fortunately other casualties were few, as the shelling was mostly directed at one portion of the wood. Meanwhile the 1st K.O.Y.L.I. who had suffered much from the shelling, beat off an infantry attack by rifle fire. Later a second attack began, reinforcements seemed necessary and "B" Coy. dashed across the open to the front line. A dip in the ground favoured the advance and the casualties were few, but Capt. Gardner was shot through the heart as he entered the trench, a great loss. He was one of the finest looking and best soldiers in the Battalion. 2/Lt. Paul was wounded about the same time.

The attack in front was beaten off and in the afternoon in the immediate neighbourhood, proved quiet, but there was great danger of the company being surrounded. The P.P.C.L.I. on the right were forced back to their support trench and on the left to the north of the wood there was a large gap and both flanks were more or less in the air. Accordingly Capt. Gattie went to the H.Q. of the Rifle Brigade, near Bellewaarde Lake, for reinforcements to protect the exposed flanks, especially to the north, and was able to guide them as far as the P.P.C.L.I. support trench, but machine-gun fire prevented them from advancing further until dark. Meanwhile a party of the Monmouths and K.O.Y.L.I. were in fact in advance of all other British troops with both flanks exposed. Towards evening the bullets of our troops, counter-attacking up the railway, were beginning to take them in the rear, so that it was clearly impossible to hold on.

The party was now completely cut off from its own Brigade, so Capt. Gattie proceeded to Brigade H.Q. for orders, leaving the remains of "B" Coy. under 2/Lt. Somerset.

Under cover of darkness the men of both units filed out of the right end of the trench and were sorted out, and the men in the wood were ordered to rejoin. This party had received no orders to advance in the morning and had been left behind. The senior soldier, Cpl. Sketchley, had kept them together during the day and now led 30 men out to join the Company. The enemy attack up the railway on his left had come so near that his party had taken a prisoner and they now brought him with them. Cpl. Sketchley received the D.C.M. for his great initiative and pluck at this period. Capt. Mallinson was awarded the D.S.O., for his fine leadership in maintaining this position and finally in extricating his party from a very difficult position.

The enemy did not attempt to harass the withdrawal and the whole mixed party got safely back to the Rifle Brigade H.Q. After a halt there they proceeded across the railway to the Potijze Road intending to rejoin the Brigade at Vlamertinghe.

At the G.H.Q. line a Staff Officer ordered the party to the trenches again, so just as dawn was breaking on the 9th they turned off the road, near the trench occupied on May 4th and advanced across open fields to the front line. There was only room on their immediate front for the K.O.Y.L.I. so the Monmouthshire party occupied some little dugouts a hundred yards in rear.

Here the remains of "B" Coy. spent the day, among them two N.C.O's who later in the war made the supreme sacrifice, Sergt. H. Lewis and Sergt. T. Howells, that fine old soldier who won the D.C.M. in the South African War and a bar to it in the Great War. Sgt. Owen of "C" Coy. joined the party during the day, also two men, who were shelled out of the buildings on the left. The enemy paid no attention to "B" Coy., probably did not know of ~~its~~ their existence, but fired heavy stuff overhead into Ypres all day. It was a day of inaction that tried the nerves far more than a day of hard fighting. Luckily it was not a day of starvation too, for early in the morning some foragers found a broken down water-cart and bread and tinned honey dumped in the road.

The casualties for the day had been enormous and the Brigade Diary records these as being 128 officers and 4,379 men killed, wounded and missing.

In the 3rd Monmouths "A" and"D" Companies had one officer and less than 30 men including those on H.Q. duties, and "B" and "C" companies had 3 officers and barely 100 men.

In the 2nd Battle of Ypres, the 3rd Monmouthshires had lost 11 officers, 2 C.S.M's., killed and 12 Officers the R.S.M. and one C.S.M. wounded. The actual casualties amongst the N.C.O's and men are difficult to state with certainty as a great number of those killed were posted as missing. As nearly as can be estimated 260 were killed and about 400 wounded. It is greatly to the honour of the Battalion that very few other than those wounded were taken prisoners. After the heavy fighting of May 8th "A" & "D" Companies were reduced to one officer and less than 30 men including those on H.Q. duties and "B" and "C" Companies to 3 officers and barely 100 men.

In the evening Lt. Merten Jones and C.S.M. Morris arrived with rations and water after they had almost walked into the German lines whilst looking for "B" Company. Some cavalry too arrived as a relief and finally on the 10th, "B" Company reached the huts at Vlamertinghe, where the rest of the Battalion had been for twenty-four hours.

During all this period the Battalion in the line were

admirably served by the transport, under Lt. Merten Jones. This officer not only displayed great courage and judgment in bringing ammunition, trench stores and rations up at night, but also in constantly reconnoitring routes up to the line by day. In this way he saved many lives and never failed us in the line. For these fine services he received a mention and the French Croix de Guerre.

The method of feeding troops in the line was for rations to be delivered in bulk to the Quartermaster's Stores and there packed in sandbags, six rations to a bag and twelve bags to a pony, the bags tied together for ease of carriage by man or horse. Water was taken up in water-carts and ammunition and trench stores in limbers or G.S. wagons. The C.Q.M.S. of each company was in charge of his company's rations. He used to report with his party every night at his company headquarters and act as postman both ways, a welcome figure from the outside world.

All transport from Ypres had to come through the Menin Gate and along either the Menin Road of Zonnebeke Road and had to dodge the bursts of German shelling. The Quartermaster's Stores were at first in Ypres in the Boulevard Malou, but the heavy shelling at the end of April drove them out of this place and after various moves finally back to Poperinghe, and only the first line transport remained billetted in a field west of Ypres.

The confused fighting of the early days of May naturally involved the transport. A few days before the retirement from the Polygon Wood orders were received to take up two day's rations in bulk besides the day's rations in bags. C.Q.M.S. Leeson was entrusted with this duty and had the rations in A.S.C. wagons; his orders were to dump them off the main road just east of Frezenberg from which point ponies were to take them up to the dump by the Polygon

Wood. Unfortunately one of the wagons fell into a shell hole as far back as Potijze Chateau, two miles from the destined dump, and all hands had to work all night to get the rations up. The sun was rising by the time the job was finished, but a kindly mist came to our aid and the German gunner, ever a man of routine, was sure that no transport was on the road at 3 a.m. so betook himself to sleep or breakfast.

The retirement added greatly to the Transport Officer's difficulties, even Brigade was not too sure of the whereabouts of battalions and companies and reconnaissances was needed before ration parties could be sent forward. The line was by no means continuous and on May 8th Capt. Walker, the York & Lancaster Regt., the senior transport officer of the Brigade who had with him C.Q.M.S. Morris & Dunn of "B" and "C" companies of the 3rd Monmouths, and a string of pack mules, advanced between gaps in our own line almost up to the enemy. Fortunately the ponies were successfully retired from the rear and no harm done. This was indeed a night of confusion, for the transport could ~~not~~ find no 3rd Monmouths anywhere, and finally gave their rations to a battalion of Warwicks who had been hurried up by bus and had nothing but iron rations.

The story of the second battle, necessarily told in a fragmentary manner, now draws to a close. On the morning of May 10th all that was left of the 3rd Monmouths was collected at the huts at Vlamertinghe. They had gone through much since April 17th; the fighting of the last week was an experience that the whole ~~xxxxx~~ course of the Great War could hardly surpass. Now there was time to learn and to regret our losses but everyone at Vlamertinghe had cause to be thankful that he was alive and that so many of his comrades were spared.

The 1st Monmouths, 84th Brigade, who were also at

Vlamertinghe, only mustered three officers and 130 other ranks. The whole of the 83rd Brigade was reduced to 600 men. A battalion was formed of these remnants and Col. Gough was put in command. Capt. Gattie commanded the 3rd Monmouths and Capt. Steel the East Yorks, who had no officers of their own left. The same evening this composite battalion took over a piece of the G.H.Q. line in front of Potijze Chateau and remained for twenty-four hours till relieved by the Queen's Bays of the First Cavalry Division on the night of the 11th. The 3rd Monmouths had few casualties on the 11th, but amongst them was the C.O. who was wounded. He proceeded to hospital and Major Bridge took over the command. The Battalion moved on the night of the 11th to a bivouac in fields east of Poperinghe. Here, piles of parcels, which could not be got up to the line during the battle, awaited us, many alas ! addressed to men who had no further need of parcels. The remains of the 3rd Monmouths were now organised into two companies, Captain Gattie taking command of what was left of "A" and "B", and Captain Steel taking "C" & "D".

On the 14th a move was made west into France to the village of Winnezeele. Here the battalion remained resting and reorganised till the 22nd and a few officers were able to have a short leave. On May 21st the G.O.C.-in-C., Sir John French, inspected the Brigade and made the following speech with which this chapter may fitly close.

" I came over to say a few words to you and to tell you "how much I, as Commander-in-Chief of this Army, appreciate "the splendid work that you have all done during the recent "fighting. You have fought the Second Battle of Ypres, which "will rank amongst the most desperate and hardest fights of "the war. You may have thought, because you were not attack-"ing the enemy, that you were not helping to shorten the war. "On the contrary, by your splendid endurance and bravery "you have done a great deal to shorten it. In this, the "Second Battle of Ypres, the Germans tried by every means "in their power to get possession of that unfortunate town. "They concentrated large forces of troops and artillery, "and further than this, they had recourse to that mean and "dastardly practice hitherto unheard of in civilised warfare, "namely the use of asphyxiating gases. You have performed "the most difficult, arduous and terrific task of withstanding "a stupendous bombardment of heavy artillery, probably the "fiercest artillery fire ever directed against troops, and "warded off the enemy's attacks with magnificent bravery. "By your steadiness and devotion both the German plans were "frustrated. He was ~~xxxxxxxxxxx~~ unable to get possession "of Ypres - if he had done this, he would probably have "succeeded in preventing neutral powers from intervening - "and he was also unable to distract us from delivering our "attack in conjunction with the French in the Arras - "Armentieres district. Had you failed to repulse his attacks "and made it necessary for more troops to be sent to your "assistance, our operations in the south might not have "been able to take place and would certainly not have been "as successful as they may have been. Your Colours have "many famous names emblazoned on them, but none will be "more famous or more well deserved than that of the Second "Battle of Ypres. I want you one and all to understand how "thoroughly I realise and appreciate what you have done. I "wish to thank you, each officer, non-commissioned officer, "and man for the services you have rendered by doing your "duty so magnificently, and I am sure that your Country "will thank you too."

-X-X-X-X-

ON HIS MAJESTY'S SERVICE.

2 Freyenburg Ridge looking West

Forward slope down which C Co 3rd Monmouths reinforced 2nd East Yorks (May 5. 1915) in ~~Ba~~ broad daylight : direction = red arrow

Front line = dotted red.

Freyenburg N-S Crossroad = Man driving sheep. Railway = telegraph post ~~at~~ middle flock of sheep.

See pages 44-46 in Monmouth History

10 Mouse Trap Farm Wultje.

Front Line = dotted red

Held by 2nd Northumberland Fus and
2nd Monmouths May 8. 15

Note, front line here begins to
take the reverse slope,

7

3rd Monmouth Front Line (dotted red) looking south towards Westhoek on flank. Railway in distance.

3 Freyenberg Ridge Looking West

Forward slope down which A Co 3rd Monmouths attempted to reinforce 5th Kings Own on May 5th 1915. They reached road as indicated by red arrow. Road = N-S road through Freyenberg. Building on Skyline = "Grey Ruin" Dotted line = front line

See page ~~44-46~~ 47 in Monmouth History

5

3rd Monmouth Front Line (dotted red) May 5-8 1915 looking SE. Broodseinde Ridge on Skyline. Zonnebeke Railway (with tram) proceeding to Ypres)

E17

6 (b) 3rd Monmouth Front Line dotted red
Open to enfilade fire from Westhoek
on flank and higher ground.
Looking North from Westhoek side of
Railway – Frezenberg on Skyline.

4 Freyenberg Level Crossing looking NNE

3rd Monmouth Front Line = red dotted line beyond railway.
Monmouths attempted to reinforce 1st York & Lancs across this level crossing on May 5.15 (see page 46 in History) as indicated by red arrow.

83rd Bde.
28th Div.

Amalgamated with 1st & 2nd Mobmouths 27.5.15.

& became part of 84th Bde.

3rd MONMOUTHS

M A Y

1 9 1 5

3rd Bn: MONMOUTHSHIRE Regt- I

Instructions regarding War Diaries and Intelligence Summaries are contained in F. S. Regs., Part II. and the Staff Manual respectively. Title pages will be prepared in manuscript.

WAR DIARY
or
INTELLIGENCE SUMMARY.
(Erase heading not required.)

Army Form C. 2118.

Hour, Date, Place	Summary of Events and Information	Remarks and references to Appendices
MAY 1915		
1st May ZONNEBEEKE	Still holding same line in POLYGON WOOD.	
2nd "	Trench stores carried out of trenches in readiness for withdrawal.	
3rd "	Orders received as to withdrawal to subsidiary line about FREZENBERG. Withdrew from POLYGON WOOD about 9 AM. Lieut Bennett and 20 men 'C' Coy and Lieut Reed and 20 men 'A' Coy left behind to cover retirement. Proceeded to GHQ lines at POTIZE passing through subsidiary line which was occupied by sister Battalions.	
4th "	Shelled in GHQ line.	
	About 6 pm. 'A' Coy sent to support 5th KINGS OWN and placed in support dug outs. 'B' Coy sent to support YORK & LANCS and took over front line trenches on right of 83rd Brigade relieving KRR.	
	'C' Coy sent to support 5th KINGS OWN and placed in support dug outs.	
	'D' Coy and HD QRS remained at POTIZE.	
5th "	Front line trenches of whole Brigade very violently bombarded.	
	'A' Coy attempted to reinforce 5th KINGS OWN fire trench but were held up by machine Gun fire.	
	'C' Coy reinforced EAST YORKS in fire trench under heavy Machine Gun fire in the afternoon but were withdrawn at dusk.	
	'D' Coy and HD QRS still remained at POTIZE.	
6th "	Bombardment of trenches but not so severely.	
7th "	Bombardment resumed.	
	'B' Coy relieved in fire trench by K.O.Y.L.I. and proceeded to wood 100 yds in rear in support.	
8th "	Violent bombardment from about 4 AM - 9 AM and was followed by an attack by the enemy along the whole line.	Battalion lost heavily under Shell, Machine & Rifle Fire
	'B' Coy advanced to fire trench in support of KOYLI and with them held the front line until dusk when both flanks being in the air a withdrawal was effected.	
9th " VLAMERTINGHE.	Remnants of Battalion returned to huts near VLAMERTINGHE.	
	Spent in huts near VLAMERTINGHE. Battalion mustered.	

(73989) W4141—463. 400,000. 9/14. H.&J.Ltd. Forms/C. 2118/10.

3rd Bn Mons Regt

II

WAR DIARY
or
INTELLIGENCE SUMMARY.

(*Erase heading not required.*)

Army Form C. 2118.

Instructions regarding War Diaries and Intelligence Summaries are contained in F. S. Regs., Part II. and the Staff Manual respectively. Title pages will be prepared in manuscript.

Hour, Date, Place 1915	Summary of Events and Information	Remarks and references to Appendices
10th May. POTIJZE	Composite Battalion composed of remnants of 83rd Brigade under Lieut Col H WORSLEY GOUGH went up to trenches, 3rd Mons detachment being put in G H Q line at POTIJZE.	
11th " VLAMERTINGHE	Composite Battalion relieved by Cavalry (3rd Mons detachment relieved by Queens Bays) Proceeded back to billets near VLAMERTINGHE. Lieut Col. H. WORSLEY GOUGH went to hospital. Major W. S. BRIDGE took over command.	
12th May POPERINGHE	Moved to camping ground near POPERINGHE and bivouacked there. Battalion organised with Coys:- No 1 (A.B) Capt. Gattie Commanding. No 2 (C.D) " Steel "	
13th "	Men had baths at POPERINGHE by Companies.	
14th " WINNEZEELE	Moved by buses at about 8 am to WINNEZEELE. Transport going on in in advance. Battalion billeted in WINNEZEELE	
15th "	Reorganization and Reequipment commenced. [Captains Steel, Gattie and Lieut Jones proceeded on 5 days leave	
16th " 20th May.	Resting – reorganising and reequipment.	
21st "	F. M. Sir John French inspected and congratulated 83rd Brigade	
22nd "	Route March by Companies. Battalion transferred to 84th Brigade	
23rd POPERINGHE	Orders received re amalgamation of 3 Monmouthshire Regts. (Battalions) Church parade. Moved by march route to wood East of POPERINGHE Joined at wood by 1st Monmouths	
24th May. VLAMERTINGHE	1st & 3rd Battalions stood to arms at dawn and shortly after moved by concealed route to HUTS at VLAMERTINGHE. Thence about midday to support trenches by lakes at ZILLEBEEKE under	

3rd Bn Mons Regt

III

Instructions regarding War Diaries and Intelligence Summaries are contained in F. S. Regs., Part II. and the Staff Manual respectively. Title pages will be prepared in manuscript.

WAR DIARY
or
INTELLIGENCE SUMMARY.

(*Erase heading not required.*)

Army Form C. 2118.

Hour, Date, Place	Summary of Events and Information	Remarks and references to Appendices
24th May	Heavy shellfire	
25th " VLAMERTINGHE	Received orders at 1 a.m. to support Counter attack by 84th Brigade. Proceeded to do so but orders countermanded about 1.45 am. Remained by lakes for rest of day at dusk returned to wood near VLAMERTINGHE	
26th May	Rested at Wood.	
27th "	Joined by 2nd Monmouths. The 3 Monmouthshire Bns were amalgamated as "The Monmouthshire Regt" under Command of Major W. S. Bridge.	
28th " HERSEELE	Battalion proceeded by march route to HERSEELE.	

W S Bridge Major
Comdg. 3rd Bn Mons Regt
28 May 1915

(73989) W4141—463. 400,000. 9/14. H.&J.Ltd. Forms/C. 2118/10.

83rd Bde.
28th Div.

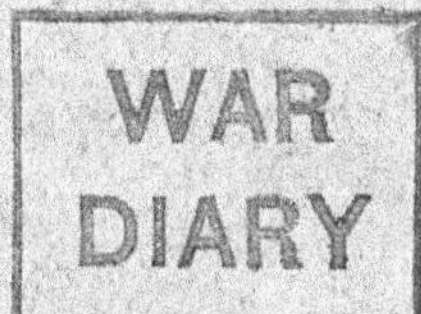

Ceased to be amalgamated with 1st & 2nd Battalions after 11th August & rejoined 83rd Bde as :-

3rd M O N M O U T H S

A U G U S T

1 9 1 5

On His Majesty's Service.

1st & 3rd (Composite) Battalion, Monmouthshire Regt

WAR DIARY
or
~~INTELLIGENCE SUMMARY~~
(*Erase heading not required.*)

Army Form C. 2118

Instructions regarding War Diaries and Intelligence Summaries are contained in F. S. Regs., Part II. and the Staff Manual respectively. Title Pages will be prepared in manuscript.

Place	Date	Hour	Summary of Events and Information	Remarks and references to Appendices
LINDENHOEK	1.8.15		Enemy quiet a mine exploded in G1 which caught the German mine which had reached our parapet. Squeals and shouts were heard from underground. Lieut Bayley was responsible for this successful counter mining which probably saved the trench G1 held by the Northumberland Fusiliers. Some "Coal boxes" over but no casualties. The garrison of the line is very weak and at night the men are on an hour and off an hour and all men including Officers servants and sanitary Police etc doing duty. Capt O W D Steel sick. Orders for relief on night of 2nd & 3rd. 2/Lts C. T. Vachell & R T. Llewellyn joined the Battalion.	
	2.8.15		Quiet night. Capt Wilson shot through the head while looking over the parapet and killed instantly. Battn relieved by 6th Welsh Regt commanded by Lt Col Lord Ninian-Stewart. Relief completed 1.30 a m. Marched to LOCRE	
LOCRE	3.8.15		Battalion billetted in BADAJOZ HUTS	
KEMMEL	4.8.15		Battn moved to KEMMEL SHELTERS in evening. took over from 1st Suffolk Regt. one Coy 6th Welsh Regt attached for tactical purposes.	
"	5.8.15		Battn still in KEMMEL SHELTERS. Capt Williams and Lieut G.S. Crawford joined the Battalion. Lieut S.R. Martyn went to hospital sick. Major Evill proceeded to England on 5 days leave	
"	6.8.15		Draft arrived from Base consisting of 1st Battn Lts Griffiths and Davies 2/Lieut Phillips and 93 Other Ranks 3rd Battn 2/Lt C A Stafford 2/Lieut J M Reynolds 2/Lieut W Collings and 157 Other Ranks	

1875 Wt. W593/826 1,000,000 4/15 J.B.C. & A. A.D.S.S./Forms/C. 2118.

Instructions regarding War Diaries and Intelligence Summaries are contained in F. S. Regs., Part II. and the Staff Manual respectively. Title Pages will be prepared in manuscript.

WAR DIARY
or
~~INTELLIGENCE SUMMARY~~
(Erase heading not required.)

Army Form C. 2118

Place	Date	Hour	Summary of Events and Information	Remarks and references to Appendices
LOCRE.	7 Aug 15		Battn moved to billets in LOCRE handing over to 2nd Cheshire Regt. 2/Lt J A J C Devey went to hospital sick.	
	8.8.15.		Church Parade for all denominations except R.Co.	
"	9.8.15.		General reorganisation to prepare for the transfer of the 3rd Mons to 83rd Brigade. Billets partly changed by Brigade Order but the Battalion still in LOCRE the readjustment of being changed caused by a Brigade of "Kitchener's Army" being in the district. A detachment of 1st Mons machine gunners ordered to take over SP8 & SP9 taking over our own guns, the present guns being left with the 6th Welsh Regt.	
"	10.8.15		Battalion still in billets in LOCRE.	
"	11.8.15		Paraded at 6.30 am to re-organise, 1st Monmouths for trench duty and again at 11 am. Lt-Col Bridge attended this parade to wish 1st Mons. Good bye. 3rd Battn paraded at 3 pm and Brig. Gen Bols was also present to wish them Good bye on leaving the 84th Bde. After which they marched off to join 83rd Bde. Both Battns again establish their identity as from this parade. Major Evill returned from leave and assumed command of 1st Monmouths. New quarters of 3rd Battn were in a meadow near LOCRE on the slope of MONT ROUGE. The Battn settled down in bivouacs. Reorganisation & training of specialists. Capt A G Newman reported for duty & relinquished the temporary rank of Captain on joining.	

1875 Wt. W593/826 1,000,000 4/15 J.B.C. & A. A.D.S.S./Forms/C. 2118.

3rd Battalion Monmouth Regt.

WAR DIARY
or
~~INTELLIGENCE SUMMARY~~
(Erase heading not required.)

Army Form C. 2118

Instructions regarding War Diaries and Intelligence Summaries are contained in F. S. Regs., Part II. and the Staff Manual respectively. Title Pages will be prepared in manuscript.

Place	Date	Hour	Summary of Events and Information	Remarks and references to Appendices
LOCRE	12.8.15		Lieut L. D. Whitehead (from 4th Entrenching Battalion) rejoined. One man was wounded on working party	
"	14.8.15		Capt O. W. D. Steel proceeded on 5 days leave to England	
	16.8.15		A draft of 30 Other Ranks joined the Battalion	
	17.8.15		2 Lieut J. H. J. Dewey rejoined from Hospital	
"	18.8.15		Owing to Captain Steel's ill health notification was received that his leave indefinitely extended.	
"	21.8.15		Coy Commanders & M. G. Officer reconnoitred the trenches which the Battn was under orders to relieve on the following day & which were new to the Battn. Lt Findlay was admitted to hospital sick. Lt J. O. Carpenter temporarily took over the transport	
"	22.8.15		The Battn relieved 5th King's Own in trenches G4 H1. H2 H3 and corresponding support and reserve trenches. The relief was effected without casualty. Headquarters in KEMMEL	
KEMMEL	23.8.15		Some whizzbangs & Coalboxes fell near H trenches & SP11 but did no damage. Pte Holmes was wounded in foot on carrying party	
"	24.8.15		During the night a German working party was observed from H1A and were dispersed by rapid fire. They resumed work under cover of mist during early hours of 25th and were again dispersed. 'C' Company claimed to have inflicted some casualties especially as the Germans attempted retaliation with whizzbangs. Lieut B. L. Jones was admitted to hospital	
	25.8.15			

1875 Wt. W593/826 1,000,000 4/15 J.B.C. & A. A.D.S.S./Forms/C. 2118.

Instructions regarding War Diaries and Intelligence Summaries are contained in F. S. Regs., Part II. and the Staff Manual respectively. Title Pages will be prepared in manuscript.

WAR DIARY
or
~~INTELLIGENCE SUMMARY~~
(Erase heading not required.)

Army Form C. 2118

Place	Date	Hour	Summary of Events and Information	Remarks and references to Appendices
KEMMEL	26.8.15		During the night 25th & 26th 'C' Company again interfered with a German working party. Enemy probably relieved during the night 26th & 27th	
"	27.8.15		Enemy artillery shelled S.P 11	
"	28.8.15		Fairly heavy shelling by enemy. At night relieved by 5th Kings Own. Relief completed by 1. A.M without casualty. Battn marched back to Old billets at LOCRE	
LOCRE	29.8.15		Battn rested all day. At night found working party of 350 men. 3118 Pte B. Taylor was fatally wounded by G.S wound in head.	
"	30.8.15		Battn rested in billets. Had baths at WESTOUTRE	
"	31.8.15		Battn rested. The following congratulatory remarks made by an R.E Officer was received from 83rd Brigade:- "I would like to bring to your notice the excellent way in which the Working parties, supplied last night by 83rd Brigade, for work on the Subsidiary line, carried out their tasks. The working parties were I believe supplied by 3rd Monmouth Regt. Not only did the men work exceptionally well, but they did so with such good spirit that even towards the ends of their tasks (which in some cases were completed well under the estimated time) they had not the appearance of being tired. This is especially satisfactory, in view of the fact - as I was informed - the men had only just come out of the trenches. The tasks were well up to the average as to size, according to the general standard as laid down by you."	

1875 Wt. W593/826 1,000,000 4/15 J.B.C. & A. A.D.S.S./Forms/C. 2118.

83rd Bde.
28th Div.

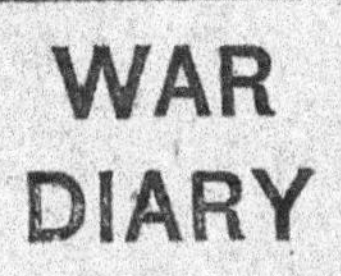

Became Pioneers to 49th Division 18.9.15.

3rd MONMOUTHS

SEPTEMBER

1 9 1 5

Army Form C. 2118

Instructions regarding War Diaries and Intelligence Summaries are contained in F. S. Regs., Part II. and the Staff Manual respectively. Title Pages will be prepared in manuscript.

WAR DIARY
or
INTELLIGENCE SUMMARY
(Erase heading not required.)

Place	Date	Hour	Summary of Events and Information	Remarks and references to Appendices
LOCRE	SEPT^R^ 1st		Battalion was employ'd as a working party.	
	2nd		Orders received to join 49th Division at A15 b Sheet 28, as Divisional Troops	
		4.0pm	Major General Bulfin (28th Division) saw the Officers of the Battalion, and asked them to convey to all ranks, his apreciation of the excellent work done, and the fine reputation which the Regiment had made for itself during the time it had served with the 28th Division	
	3rd		Battalion moved to a wood in A15 b (Sheet 28) via Reninghelst and Poperinghe. Battalion billetted in tents.	
	4th		Battalion rested in billets.	
ELVERDINGE CHATEAU	5th		Battalion moved by march route to ELVERDINGE CHATEAU grounds, billetted in tents, with H^d^ Q^rs^ in the Chateau	
	6th		Company Commanders daily inspection; Battalion employed as working party	
	7th		A few small shells fell near the Chateau. Employed as working party	
	8th		Heavy shelling all day, about 12 shells fell near Chateau. Employed as working party	
	9th		Heavy shelling, about 20 shells fell near the Chateau; one shell exploded in a room on the Ground floor. Battalion employed as a working party	

1875 Wt. W593/826 1,000,000 4/15 J.B.C. & A. A.D.S.S./Forms/C. 2118.

Army Form C. 2118

Instructions regarding War Diaries and Intelligence Summaries are contained in F. S. Regs., Part II. and the Staff Manual respectively. Title Pages will be prepared in manuscript.

WAR DIARY
or
INTELLIGENCE SUMMARY
(Erase heading not required.)

Place	Date SEPT^R	Hour	Summary of Events and Information	Remarks and references to Appendices
ELVERDINGE CHATEAU	10th		Heavy shelling by artillery. Battalion employed as working party.	
	11th		Heavy shelling by French artillery. Battalion on working party.	
	12th		Quiet day, no shelling. Battalion employed as working party.	
	13th		Exceptionally quiet day. Battalion employed as working party. 2751 [illegible] Pte W.T. was wounded (GS) in head.	
	14th		Few shells fell near Chateau. Battalion employed as working party.	
	15th		Battalion employed as working party.	
	16th		Shells fell around the Chateau. Battalion employed as working party.	
	17th		Battalion employed as working party.	
	18th		Battalion is to be the Pioneer Battalion of the 49th Division, from this date.	
	19th		Battalion commenced a new drainage scheme at BRIELEN. This work is being carried out by reliefs, of two companies, on alternate nights.	
	20th		Quiet day. Battalion found working parties.	

1875 Wt. W593/826 1,000,000 4/15 J.B.C. & A. A.D.S.S./Forms/C. 2118.

Instructions regarding War Diaries and Intelligence Summaries are contained in F. S. Regs., Part II. and the Staff Manual respectively. Title Pages will be prepared in manuscript.

WAR DIARY
or
INTELLIGENCE SUMMARY
(Erase heading not required.)

Army Form C. 2118

Place	Date	Hour	Summary of Events and Information	Remarks and references to Appendices
	SEPT.R			
ELVERDINGE CHATEAU	21st		Orders received from 49th Division, that 180 men would move to dug-outs on the Canal Bank. Two companies were detailed to take up these billets accordingly.	
	22nd		Battalion on working parties. 2901 Pte Perry C. was fatally wounded (G.S.) in L breast.	
	23rd		Quiet day. No working parties found by the Battalion.	
	24th		Major W.A. Lewis rejoined the Battalion, as second in command, and 2/Lieut C. Raymont joined for duty.	
	25th		Quiet day. Battalion found working parties. 1868 Sergt Hookham was slightly wounded (G.S) in Scalp.	
	26th		Working parties were found. At night a few shells fell near Chateau.	
	27th		Two Companies relieved the 180 men at Canal Bank. The relieved party return'd to the Chateau grounds at 3·30pm.	
	28th		Battalion found working parties.	
	29th		A few Shells fell near the Chateau. Battalion found working parties. 1430 Pte Pearce was kill'd by a shell, and 167 Pte Legge was wounded by a shell; both casualties being at the Canal Bank.	

1875 Wt. W593/826 1,000,000 4/15 J.B.C. & A. A.D.S.S./Forms/C. 2118.

Army Form C. 2118

Instructions regarding War Diaries and Intelligence Summaries are contained in F. S. Regs., Part II. and the Staff Manual respectively. Title Pages will be prepared in manuscript.

WAR DIARY
or
INTELLIGENCE SUMMARY
(Erase heading not required.)

Place	Date SEPT^R	Hour	Summary of Events and Information	Remarks and references to Appendices
ELVERDINGE CHATEAU	30th		Battalion found usual working parties.	
			A draft of 34, joined the Battalion from the Base.	
			2577 Pte Ashton. R. was fatally wounded (G.S) in the heart.	

Pioneers.
49th Division.

Came from 83rd Bde. 28th Div. 18.9.15

3rd M O N M O U T H S

O C T O B E R

1 9 1 5

On His Majesty's Service.

Instructions regarding War Diaries and Intelligence Summaries are contained in F. S. Regs., Part II. and the Staff Manual respectively. Title Pages will be prepared in manuscript.

WAR DIARY
or
INTELLIGENCE SUMMARY
(Erase heading not required.)

Army Form C. 2118

Place	Date 1915 October	Hour	Summary of Events and Information	Remarks and references to Appendices
ELVERDINGE CHATEAU	1st		Battalion found usual working parties, for drainage work, with R.E.s	
	2nd		Battalion found usual day and night working parties.	
	3rd		2 Coys relieved the two companies, at Canal Dugouts. Relief completed at 4 pm.	
	4th		Usual working parties were found. 2/Lts A J Ratcliffe, J. F. Rees R. G. Davies, joined the Battalion for duty, from England.	
			2305 Pt. Skinn E. J. was slightly wounded by shrapnel, in head.	
	5th		Usual working parties were found. Arrangements were made with 5 Batt West York Regt, to exchange Dugouts, at Canal Bank, so that the detached working party would be nearer the work upon which they are engaged.	
	6th		Usual working parties were found. 2/Lt A. J. Wood, joined the Battalion for duty.	
	7th		Battalion employed as working parties.	
	8th		Battalion employed as working parties.	
	9th		Usual working parties were found. 2 Coys relieved the two companies at the Canal Dugouts. Relief completed at 4.30 pm.	
	10th		Battalion employed as working parties.	
	11th		Usual working parties found. The exchange of Dugouts, arranged on the 5th took place; and completed by 5 pm.	
	12th		Battalion employed as working parties. A few shells fell near the CHATEAU in the afternoon and evening.	

1875 Wt. W593/826 1,000,000 4/15 J.B.C. & A. A.D.S.S./Forms/C. 2118.

Army Form C. 2118

WAR DIARY
or
INTELLIGENCE SUMMARY

(Erase heading not required.)

Instructions regarding War Diaries and Intelligence Summaries are contained in F. S. Regs., Part II. and the Staff Manual respectively. Title Pages will be prepared in manuscript.

Place	Date 1915 October	Hour	Summary of Events and Information	Remarks and references to Appendices
ELVERDINGHE	13th		Battalion employed as working parties.	
CHATEAU	14th		Usual working parties were found.	
	15th		Usual working parties were found.	
	16th		Battalion employed as working parties. 1045 Pt. Smith B, wounded (G.S) in shoulder.	
	17th		Battalion employed as working party. 2625 Pt. Winney A. wounded (G.S) in shoulder.	
	18th		Usual working parties were found. A few shells fell near the CHATEAU, about 9.30 pm.	
	19th		Battalion found usual working parties.	
	20th		Usual working parties were found.	
	21st		2 Coys relieved the two companies at Canal Dugouts. Relief completed at 4.30 pm.	
	22nd		Battalion employed as working parties.	
			Lt. B.L. Jones rejoined Battalion, after being invalided to England.	
			847 Pt. Blake C. wounded (G.S) Trunk. 2991 Pt Lampard A. wounded (shrapnel) Shoulder.	
			Extract London Gazette. 19.x.15. To be Tempy Capt. Lt. W.P. Abbott. d/ Aug 1st 1915.	
	23rd		Battalion found working parties. " " " Lt. A.G. Newman d/ Sept 10th 1915.	
	24th		Battalion found usual working parties. Elverdinghe shelled about midnight and early in the morning. Few shells fell near Chateau.	
			2/Lt. Vaughan Lewis goes to Hospital.	
	25th		Battalion found usual working parties. 1264 Pt Bird C. wounded (GS) Nose.	
	26th		Battalion employed as working parties. 2/Lt. Vaughan Lewis, returned from Hospital.	

1875 Wt. W593/826 1,000,000 4/15 J.B.C. & A. A.D.S.S./Forms/C. 2118.

Army Form C. 2118

Instructions regarding War Diaries and Intelligence Summaries are contained in F. S. Regs., Part II. and the Staff Manual respectively. Title Pages will be prepared in manuscript.

WAR DIARY
or
INTELLIGENCE SUMMARY
(Erase heading not required.)

Place	1915 Date October	Hour	Summary of Events and Information	Remarks and references to Appendices
ELVERDINGHE CHATEAU	27th		Battalion found the usual working parties.	
			The Commanding Officer Lt Col. W.S. Bridge with 20. O.R. proceeded to ABEELE, and represented the Battalion in an inspection of the Corps, by H.M. the King.	
			The following message was received from the Army Commander. "His Majesty the King desires me to say, that he was very pleased with the soldierly bearing of the troops, and with all he saw of the Second Army today". 3235 Pte Morgan. C. wounded	
	28th		Usual working parties were found.	
			24 N.C.O's and men proceeded to R.E. Farm, for employment as Carpenters, under R.E.	
	29th		Battalion employed as working parties. 2588. Cpl. Morrell D. wounded (GS) Thigh	
	30th		Battalion found usual working parties.	
	31st		Battalion employed as working parties.	
			A draft of 74 N.C.O's and men, joined the Battalion from the Base	
			1154. Sergt. Lewis. H.G. was wounded (GS) in arm and Thigh.	

www.ingramcontent.com/pod-product-compliance
Lightning Source LLC
Chambersburg PA
CBHW081541160426
43191CB00011B/1811

* 9 7 8 1 4 7 4 5 1 4 2 3 1 *